Take It from Me

Take It from Me

Life's a Struggle But You Can Win

Erin Brockovich
with Marc Eliot

McGraw-Hill

NEW YORK   CHICAGO   SAN FRANCISCO   LISBON   LONDON
MADRID   MEXICO CITY   MILAN   NEW DELHI   SAN JUAN   SEOUL
SINGAPORE   SYDNEY   TORONTO

McGraw-Hill

A Division of The **McGraw·Hill** *Companies*

1 2 3 4 5 6 7 8 9 0   DOC/DOC   0 9 8 7 6 5 4 3 2 1

ISBN 0-07-138379-4

This book was set in Times New Roman by North Market Street Graphics.

Printed and bound by R. R. Donnelley & Sons Company.

McGraw-Hill books are available at special quantity discounts to use as premiums and sales promotions, or for use in corporate training programs. For more information, please write to the Director of Special Sales, Professional Publishing, McGraw-Hill, Two Penn Plaza, New York, NY 10121-2298. Or contact your local bookstore.

 This book is printed on recycled, acid-free paper containing a minimum of 50% recycled, de-inked fiber.

To the victims in Hinkley, who helped inspire me and became my heroes

Contents

Take It from Me

PART ONE

Before Hinkley and After the Movie

I'm the *Real* Erin Brockovich, and My Life Is No Big-Screen Fairy Tale!

*B*elieve me when I tell you I've never experienced anything stranger and more wondrous than seeing my reflection idealized in the movies. The film that bore my name and starred the glamorous Julia Roberts in a performance for which she won an Academy Award playing me was in many ways the cherry on the top of the chocolate cake of my life, a life that had not always been so sweet and creamy.

The movie focused primarily on the work I did for the law firm of Masry and Vititoe in the direct action they brought against the Pacific Gas and Electric (PG&E) Utility Corporation on behalf of the citizens of Hinkley, California. Working together, we were able to show how PG&E had for years been polluting the town's drinking water with chromium 6, which PG&E used as an anticorrosive inhibitor in their pumping plant's cooling towers. Wastewater from the plant was being dumped on the desert floor into unlined ponds from which it was leaching into the acquifer that was the town's drinking water. The citizens were also inhaling toxic vapors whenever they took hot showers or used this water in their swamp coolers—their primary source of air-conditioning. Their children were soaking up chromium-laced sprinkler water during the summers. Hinkley's citizens were experiencing a rash of miscarriages, unexplained nosebleeds, skin disorders, and continual animal deaths, followed by various digestive disorders and cancers.

In 1996, after four long and difficult years (which the film squeezes into a quick two hours), I found myself on the receiving end of a check for $2.5 million, my share of the unprecedented quarter-billion-dollar settlement. During all of this, in 1995, a year before the settlement, through my girlfriend Pamela Dumond, my life story was sold to Jersey Films. The film would be the first public acknowledgment of what I had been through. Because Julia agreed to play me, the film actually got made. Julia won a Best Actress Oscar for being me. Not bad, right? But wait, there's more.

After years of having to survive in a roach-infested dump (just like the one you saw Julia living in, in the film), with my bonus money I was, at last, financially strong enough to purchase what I thought was my ultimate dream house. And, after two disastrous marriage misses, I hit the bull's-eye when I married Eric, the perfect image of my ideal man. By 1997, it surely seemed as if my life had, indeed, turned into that giant slice of delicious cherry chocolate cake!

Except, as the song goes, someone must have left the cake out in the rain!

To begin with, after I moved into a new house, I discovered that much of the place was going to have to be torn down and rebuilt from scratch, due to the presence of toxic mold just about everywhere—inside the walls, above the ceilings, and below the floorboards. Besides the immediate danger to my family, the toxic mold also meant that I couldn't just sell the place and buy a new one. Who in his or her right mind would ever knowingly buy into such a health hazard? And anyway, I wouldn't think of selling it to anyone in this condition. I don't do things that way. Instead, I made the hard choice to bite the bullet and renovate the entire structure, from basement to roof, at a cost that totaled about as much as I originally paid for the whole thing.

And you know what? I didn't really care! It didn't matter to me one bit because I am not my house. The new house is simply okay, a *place* to sleep with four walls and a roof, and that's all. Whatever happens in the end with it, even if I never see a penny from the lawsuit I have going against the contractors, it's still and always will be just a house. If it costs a million dollars to rebuild, which it probably will, that's okay too. I'll just figure out another way to make some more money. My only concern is that my children have a safe roof over their heads. Whether it's a palace or a dump—and we've lived in both—I will provide for them.

> I am not my house.

After all, they are totally my responsibility. I've told Eric, my third husband, that the children's issues are and always will be my burden, not his. They are *my* children. They are *my* responsibility, and have been for a very long time. I learned that reality when I went through all the usual hassles of collecting child support, often only to hear, "I'm broke."

After too many years of hassling with my exes, one day I finally decided I wasn't going to waste any more of my time hauling them in and out of court. Instead, I figured I'd take that same energy and put it into caring for the children, even if I had to do it all on my own. This didn't mean I thought it was okay for my exes to shirk their paternal responsibilities, but I had made up my mind not to try to beat a dead horse into a deeper death. If there's one thing life had taught me, it was that even if I couldn't control anyone else's destiny, and I obviously couldn't with these two, I sure as hell could control my own.

> Even if I couldn't control anyone else's destiny, and I obviously couldn't with these two, I sure as hell could control my own.

This was a big revelation for me, one that had been a long time coming. It was part of a series of decisions I had made over the past 10 years that changed everything about the way I had decided to live my life. These changes were all part of the realization that slowly came upon me, the result of a series of events. It took me a while, but I finally figured out that the key to winning any battle has less to do with those things that happen around me than with those changes that take place *on the inside.* How these changes occurred—well, that's what I want to tell you about.

Since the film's release, people I've never met have come to me and said extraordinary (and sometimes extraordinarily silly) things, and others have written absurd things about me, mostly dealing with how "lucky" I am, or blessed, or how I've managed to live the life of some kind of real-life Cinderella. So let me start by getting something clear right from the get-go: No one's real life—especially mine—is a fairy tale, no matter how much we think it might be, or must be, or want it to be.

I, for one, run as fast as I can in the other direction whenever I hear the term "fairy princess" tossed my way. First of all, I automatically think of our last several "fairy princesses" and what fate had in store for them. Lady Diana is the first to come to mind. She was everyone's perfect female role model, until after her untimely death when we all discovered that, hey,

> The key to winning any battle has less to do with those things that happen around me than with those changes that take place on the inside.

> No one's real life—especially mine—is a fairy tale, no matter how much we think it might be, or must be, or want it to be.

maybe she wasn't such a happy princess after all. With all that wealth, beauty, and status, she could not save herself from the harder emotional realities of life. For another generation it was the first lady of Camelot, Jackie Kennedy Onassis. For others, it was the screen goddess Marilyn Monroe. All of them, and so many more, serviced our fantasies while living far more difficult, less emotionally fulfilling lives.

So let's not fall so easily for this mythic notion of perfect fairy princesses. I don't care who you are—how rich, how beautiful, how cultured, or congenial. On some level life will always be a struggle, one you may either win or lose, no matter how many advantages or disadvantages you bring to the table. Winning that struggle is what's really important—not how much money you have, or fame, or what you're wearing in that photo in the newspaper, what designer has dressed you, or who's done your hair. (And just to help keep everything in perspective, since the Hinkley case was settled, 50 of the original 634 plaintiffs have died from causes we now believe were related to the presence of chromium 6 in their drinking water. So all the money and recognition they got from the film didn't do them a lot of good either.)

Here is an Erin Brockovich reality check: Since I earned my $2.5 million bonus, I have paid more than a million dollars in taxes, I will spend more than a million to save my house, I have fought off "formers" and "exes" who wanted a piece of what I had earned and that they weren't entitled to, *and I have spent more than a quarter of a million dollars on rehab treatment for my two oldest children.*

That's right. Matt, my oldest, was fourteen when he started experimenting with drugs, which alarmed me, as I have been against drugs my entire life. Katie was only thirteen when she started. Both were unable to escape the peer pressures everywhere in teenage America today. No matter how upscale and isolated you think your neighborhood is, and the one I moved into is about as upscale

> Winning that struggle is what's really important—not how much money you have, or fame, or what you're wearing in that photo in the newspaper, what designer has dressed you, or who's done your hair.

and isolated as it gets, believe me, drugs are there.

That part of the drug problem is external, and in the real world, for all intents and purposes, unavoidable. Kids today just don't have the same fear of "dope" and the debilitating addiction that so often accompanies it that we did when we were their age. Maybe it's because of all those legal drug commercials on TV, or the completely easy availability of the birth control pill, or maybe just seeing their parents popping pills for instant cures to anything and everything that ails them all day long. Or it simply could be that they're so young they think they're going to live forever. Or they think that having all the money in the world and a house in the best zip code will protect them from the killer scourge of hard drugs that flow in the streets.

However, the other part is far more difficult, first to recognize and then to deal with. It is the *internal* side. For Matt and Katie, whatever problems they've had most likely began with the divorce and absence of a father in their day-to-day lives, of any man who stayed long enough for them to think of as a "real dad." In other words, no symbol of constancy. Raising them alone, as I did, I too was away a lot, and I won't even try to deny that. I was, finally, unable to keep drugs away from them, or them away from drugs. Fortunately, Matt was strong and able to call upon his inner strength when he had to. When I arranged for professional assistance, his self-determination shined through. Today, I absolutely believe drugs are a part of his past. I am truly grateful I was able to provide him with all the help he needed and that he was able to overcome this problem.

Katie, too, is doing well. At the age of thirteen, when she first started displaying behavioral problems, compounded with O.C.D. (obsessive compulsive disorder), it was hell for all of us. For the better part of a year I didn't want to believe that I was going to have a difficult time with her as well. When I realized how serious her situation was, I found an educational consultant, who recommended a three-week, highly supervised "wilderness" program, set in the middle of Idaho. After that, I moved her into an emotional-growth boarding school in Oregon, where, in the 16 months she was there, she flourished. Toward the end of that program, she started to backslide a bit, and at the recommendation of the school, I placed Katie into another wilderness program, this time for nine weeks, in Utah. In a strange way, I was actually grateful for this diagnosis. At last, I had some form of explanation for the way she was.

One night while she was away, after hours of sleepless soul searching, I was feeling particularly helpless about the situation, both hers and mine. That's when I decided to sit down and write my daughter an "impact" letter. I based it on a philosophy my father had once shared with me, part of which was originally written by, of all people, Calvin Coolidge. I call it my "Press On" inspiration. I was so moved by it, so affected by what it said, that I've carried Dad's original letter for 20 years, everywhere I've ever gone, since the day I received it in the mail. Here, now, is some of what Dad shared with me:

> Press on. Nothing can take the place of perseverance. Talent will not. Nothing is more common than unsuccessful men with talent. Genius will not. Unrewarded genius is almost a proverb. Education will not. The world is full of

educated derelicts. Persistence and determination alone are omnipotent. This slogan, "press on," has solved, always will solve, the problems of the human race.

—Calvin Coolidge

Press on! How those two words hit home! When I first received Dad's letter, I read it over and over again, every day, until I had completely absorbed its meaning. The notion of "pressing on," no matter what, made so much sense to me, and it still does.

My dad had shared this with me because at the time I had hit a brick wall in my life, and I didn't know how to get around it. He thought there was something there I might be able to grab hold of. I was in my early twenties, with two failed marriages already behind me, and I was trying to raise two children on my own. I had no real education, and I knew that my looks were not going to be enough for me to make it as some famous model or actress. Feeling as if I had nothing to offer, I began to worry over how I was going to meet Mr. CEO, the perfect man who would love unconditionally and care for my children and me in some big fancy home. I was really down on myself, about ready to give it all up, unable or unwilling to face the hard truth that I had no one else to rely on for anything *except myself.*

> The notion of "pressing on," no matter what, made so much sense to me, and it still does.

That was why my dad shared this philosophy. He knew it was time I took control of my life, and he believed the message to "press on" would hit home. And he was right. As soon as I received it, that little-train-that-could whistle went off in my head, chugging its message over and over again: "I think I can, I think I can, I know I can, I know I can . . . !" It all started to make sense again. Take everything away, I told myself, and there's still *me,* and I have what it takes to pick myself up by my bootstraps and . . . *press on!*

It was the same message I then wanted Katie to get from me. I wanted her to realize that nobody could make her do anything, or take anything away from her, *unless she allowed them to.* I knew she could hear it, and I knew she could do it. The night I sent my version of *press on* to Katie, I added the following words at the bottom: "This has applied to our entire family. Believe it, practice it, apply it. It *works.*"

It took me a long time after receiving my dad's letter to fully understand the power and the force of this notion of "pressing on," to understand how it involved the need to find the inner strength inside myself that had always been there from the start and that was just waiting for me to figure out how to kick it into motion. Now I am confident that both Katie and Matt are receiving the same message, but only at a much earlier age. They have their own "little engine that could." They know that.

> "I think I can,
> I think I can,
> I know I can,
> I know I
> can . . . !"

*   *   *

When I first received my $2.5 million bonus, I quickly found out how ex-boyfriends and former husbands can come out of the woodwork, looking to chew into me like hungry termites. Remember Jorge, that "great guy" in the movie who "volunteered" to take care of my kids while I worked on the case? Well, things change, and people change too. Here's what *really* went down after the end credits ran.

We had been living together about a year when the Hinkley case first began to take over my life. To make sure I had the freedom I needed to work on it, Ed Masry's law firm *hired* Jorge to be my children's nanny. That's right, Jorge was *paid* to take care of the kids. At first the arrangement worked well, and he seemed like a godsend. I had already gone through three or four nannies, all of whom turned out to be nightmares. One ended up being a stalker, and another was like the Pied Piper. I would come home every night to find my house all but destroyed. Another one let the baby scream in her crib all day long until the neighbors complained to me, wondering if there weren't some sort of child abuse taking place. One night I came in late, and Beth, my youngest, who was only eighteen months old at the time, was across the street with neighbors (I figured that out by following the trail of the red Sharpie mark she left on the walls and front door). The nanny who was supposed to be caring for all three kids was locked in her room watching TV.

Jorge, the biker, meanwhile, had moved in, and was having a tough time making a go of it. He had a steady job at his father's restoration shop, but there just weren't enough hours, and then his brother, who was running the shop, began to make noise about moving the whole thing out of state. Jorge liked being with the kids, and they liked him, so Ed suggested we simply formalize the situation and offer to pay him to be their nanny. I agreed.

This came at a critical time in my work in Hinkley. I had uncovered an incredible amount of information that needed to be verified, fleshed out, followed up on, and followed through. I was beginning to identify with these good people and their massive struggle against the overwhelming odds to survive. I saw my own struggles reflected in theirs, and knew I had to devote as much of my time and effort as possible to the case. So when the biker came along, he seemed to offer the perfect solution to how to care for the kids while I pursued the situation in Hinkley.

I should tell you right here that I knew in my heart he was not my Prince Charming. While I loved that he watched the kids and appreciated what he was doing, I told him time and time again, I was not *in love* with him. And let's face it, even though he may have babysat out of the "goodness" of his heart, he was also paid for it. Every two weeks a very nice-sized check arrived for him, he was living rent free (I was still paying full rent for the place), and he had his own car provided by Ed's law firm, to make Jorge as comfortable as possible while spending his days playing with my kids. In 1997 when I finally received my settlement money and decided to buy a new house, I thought it might be a good time for the biker to move on.

It wasn't the first time I had wanted him to leave, only now I had the means to act upon it. On more than one occasion I had become so fed up with Jorge's self-important attitude and constant reminders of how crucial he was to all of us that I just finally threw him out. He never understood, or wanted to understand, that he wasn't doing us any favors and that he was only there because Ed and I had *hired* him so that I could continue to do my work.

In 1995, when I first asked him to leave, not only did he refuse to go, he got a little ugly about it. I told Ed, and he said he would arrange for the sheriff to physically escort Jorge off the premises. Fortunately, that proved unnecessary. When he realized Ed and I weren't kidding around, he finally left. Not long after, he turned around and sued me for palimony *to the tune of $3 million!* This was a life-altering event for me because it proved once and for all what I had always suspected, that he had never really been there for the children at all. The whole thing had just been a free ride for him—no more, no less. During this, I came home one day, opened the mail, and found a letter from him, along with three individual photos of the children. I thought, *whoa, he sent back their pictures! That hurt.*

Of course, the palimony case was ridiculous and frivolous. But Ed negotiated with Jorge and his attorney for a one-time so-long-Charlie "bonus" in the form of a $40,000 check to make sure he would stay away and never be able to sue me again. On top of this money, about a year later, when the Hinkley case settled and I got my bonus, I gave Jorge a $20,000 custom Harley—my way of saying thanks to him for being a part of that long struggle. When times had really been tough, he had sold his Harley to help out, and I had wanted to make that up to him.

In fact, I felt so sorry for him that when he began calling to ask for one more chance, I finally caved and said yes, he could move back in. Not because of his constant pleadings or anything like that, but because of something little Beth had said to me. I was giving her a bath one night when she looked up and asked, "Where's Jorge?"

I tried to dismiss the question, but she said, "Come on, Mom, you know who I'm talking about!"

"Well, what about him?"

"I miss him," she said.

That made me feel really bad. For *her.* Other than the biker, for most of her early years, Beth had no other stable father figure in her life, and I wondered if I wasn't acting purely out of my own personal interests rather than my children's. So I agreed to give him one more go-around. However, this time, before I allowed him back in the door, Ed insisted that Jorge sign an agreement that protected me from any and all future lawsuits.

Sadly, as soon as he was back, I knew I had made a big mistake. This arrangement was never going to work. To begin with, even though I tried to put it out of my head, I could never really forgive or forget the returning of those photographs. Not surprisingly, this last go-around proved to be a short one. Less than a month later, in May 1998, he was out the door, for good this time.

Still, both Ed and I loaned him additional money to help him get back on his feet, and he was paid a very handsome sum for the right to have his character portrayed in the film. All in all, he made out very well.

No sooner was he gone than my first husband, Shawn, from whom I'd been divorced for 12 years, asked Ed and me for $10,000 to buy a trailer. This wasn't the first time that he had come to me for help, and whenever I could, I had tried to be there for him. After all, he was the father of my first two children. I had loaned him money to get his carpet-cleaning business going. I bought him a very nice used car and gave him some furniture I no longer had any need for. I did all this despite all the hassles of child support. Still, because through the years we had remained friendly for the sake of the kids—at the time he lived nearby and visited them often—now that I felt I had the means to make his life a little easier, I figured I would do what I could for him.

At this point, I was so grateful for everything that I had been given from Hinkley that it just didn't seem right to me not to share some of it with him. I thought, perhaps foolishly, that kindness and generosity might mean something to my ex, that by doing the right thing, my actions would set a good example for him, so I helped him out.

Of course, that decision came back to bite me. As the opening of the movie approached, Shawn read a newspaper article about it and began complaining to Ed and me because he assumed he was going to be portrayed as a deadbeat dad. I tried to reason with him, another mistake on my part. "Shawn," I said, "you aren't even mentioned in the movie," which was completely true. The film never identifies him by name, and there is nothing in the film about his character. "The movie is about what happened to the people of Hinkley, California. Don't you understand that?"

The simple truth was, if he hadn't tried so hard to get in on the action, no one would ever have known who he was.

But, as I say, it was like talking to a wall. The next thing I knew, he had figured out a way to bring a thousand times more attention and focus on himself. He joined forces against me with, *of all people, Jorge!* Together these two hatched a sadly misguided extortion scheme intended to "make them rich."

Shortly after the biker left and I had set up Shawn with his trailer and carpet business, the two of them came to Ed and me with a lawyer who said that unless we paid them a total of $310,000, they were going to the press with "proof" that not only was I a bad mother but that I had slept with Ed Masry. Of course, they knew their accusations were boldface lies, and the whole scheme made me sick to my stomach. What particularly hurt was that if there were any two men besides my father, Ed Masry, and my husband Eric who knew what a good mother I was, it was Shawn and Jorge. For them to come to me after I received my bonus and say that if I didn't give them all this money they were going to "expose" me was astonishing. It was well beyond my ability to comprehend how low some people could actually go.

It was true that my two older children got into problems with drugs. But my ex never had one iota of recognition that perhaps his moving in and out of their lives contributed to the kids' problems. He failed to acknowledge that I had already spent more than a quarter of a million dollars in cash on rehab programs for my children. Had I turned my back on my kids, looked the other way, made believe none of it was going on because I chose not to see it, *then* Shawn might have been able to make a case that I was a bad mother.

But what really floored me was the twisted sense of *entitlement* my two exes had. Somewhere in the recesses of whatever passes for their minds, hearts, and souls, they actually believed they were entitled to more money from me. Neither could accept the fact that I or *any* woman could get as far as I had *without* having an affair with the boss. As far as they were concerned, I *must* have slept my way to the top. I must have cheated, and therefore what they were doing was essentially the same thing—they were just stealing from thieves. They tried to take advantage of that outdated stereotype that lends credibility to the notion that the only reason an attractive, busty, uneducated woman can succeed is by sleeping her way to success.

There were two other aspects to it all that particularly outraged me. What the hell had Ed Masry ever done to either of them except be kind and generous to them and provide them with money, jobs, and cars? And, finally *what about the children?* I mean, honestly, how did either of them think the kids were going to react when they saw the front pages of the newspapers or saw on TV that not only was I a bad mother but had also been sleeping with my boss?

The biker and my ex found a big-shot Century City lawyer, who must have been in the market for a high-profile case he hoped would provide lots of free publicity and, presumably, a host of wealthy new clients. In response to the lawsuit, the Ventura County district attorney set up a sting operation. At his direction, we agreed to meet with Shawn, Jorge, and the lawyer at an office that was bugged, with a dozen police in the next room. We handed over the cash, and the next thing they knew they were busted. All three were held on $50,000 bail and charged with suspicion of extortion.

As angry as I was, knowing they had tried to compromise my principles and had not an ounce of respect or appreciation for me, it still didn't make me feel good to see the two of them taken away in handcuffs. It was depressing to know they had been brought down by their own out-of-control greed and sheer stupidity. These were, after all, two very significant men in my life. One was the father of two of my children, and the other had been there to help out while I tried to pull my life together. It was a woefully sorry state of affairs.

Bail was set at $50,000 apiece, and a trial date was set for the fall of 2000. Eventually, the DA dismissed the charges against Shawn and Jorge, but not the lawyer. His thinking was if he tried all three, there was a chance, no matter how slim, that they'd all get off, and he wanted to nail at least one of them. I thought it was the right choice, because while it may have been true that Shawn and Jorge were greedy and stupid, the lawyer's crime was worse. He was an officer of the court, and he had to know it was wrong to go along with the whole scheme. He deserved to be prosecuted to the fullest extent of the law.

The trial finally took place in March 2001. I testified and withstood a barrage of repulsive, upsetting, insinuating questions from the defense team, intent upon impinging my integrity. After five days of deliberations, the jury found the lawyer guilty. He was fined $10,000, given a 4- to 6-month jail sentence with a 36-month formal probation period, and was permanently disbarred from practicing law. I'm sure he wishes he had never laid eyes on those two. And you know what? So do I.

I will tell you right here and now, as I would tell them to their faces if I could, that when Jorge and Shawn go to bed every night, with no media, no girlfriends, no children—they've got no one else to face but themselves. They knew what the truth was, they knew they had sold their souls right down the line to make some quick money off the hard work I had done. They both knew *exactly* what kind of mother I was and that Ed Masry was a stand-up, honest, and generous man. For two people who had supposedly been so close to me, what they didn't understand was that money had never been the motivating factor in anything I had ever done, which was why it wouldn't have made one iota of difference to me if I had to spend thousands defending myself. I would have spent every cent I had to make sure my name was clear, my reputation intact, and the truth remained just that—the truth.

* * *

As I said, I've never done *anything* just for money, and, despite what Shawn, Jorge, and their lawyer might have thought, I certainly had not gone into the Hinkley case to get rich. When I discovered that people's lives were in danger and that PG&E was the

> Money had never been the motivating factor in anything I had ever done.

cause, my only goal was to see justice served, to try to help ensure protection for all of the people of that town. After all, someone had to be held accountable for what had gone down there, and the challenge to find out who and why spoke to the heart and soul of who I am. In the beginning, everyone—including Ed Masry for a time—thought I was nuts to even think about taking them on. Believe me, the last thing anyone could have seen coming was the huge settlement and the movie that would be made out of all we accomplished.

During the four long years the case took, I constantly had to reach deep down inside myself to find the desire, the ability, and the gumption to *press on.* I had to make sure that my children had food, clothes, and a roof over their heads while I devoted 24/7 to trying to blow down the house of the big bad corporate wolf. When we finally reached the more than quarter-billion-dollar settlement, another two years would pass before we were able to collect and distribute all the money. That adds up to almost six years

> I constantly had to reach deep down inside myself to find the desire, the ability, and the gumption to press on.

of my life, during which time a lot of people dismissed my efforts as just one of Erin's crazy no-win adventures in blunderland.

It took that long for me to prove them all wrong. And victory signaled once and for all my late-blooming arrival into the world of responsible adulthood. I have to say the day of the settlement was one of the most thrilling experiences of my life. Ed and I finally had the opportunity to call some of the 634 plaintiffs and personally tell them about the settlement. There was more laughing, crying and eventually hugging than I'd seen in a very long time. That was great fun and on a certain, very profound level, quite fulfilling. For here was the final, long-awaited confirmation to me of my own self-esteem, tangible proof that I found the motivation, the strength, the endurance, and the ability to see something through to a successful end. My long struggle had resulted in a level of victory that enabled me to rediscover the essential moral and spiritual qualities I had first learned in childhood, values that I had for many years misplaced and allowed to lie dormant until they were finally reawakened by my being allowed by Ed Masry and his law firm to take on PG&E.

Because what's inside of us is not as easily or instantly recognizable as what people see on the outside, even after the case was settled, there were many people who naturally assumed (as my ex and the biker mistakenly had) that it must have been my hot-cha clothes, big chest, and presumably loose high-heels that had led me to victory. In truth, it was my identification with the victims—the unglamorous, hard-working, dirt-on-their-hands, clothes-on-the-line, early-to-bed and early-to-rise folks—that helped me understand why in my own life for such a long time it had been so difficult to ever get anyone to listen to me *about anything*. No wonder when I finally proved how a woman with my big-blonde looks and fast-times style could successfully take on PG&E and win that *People* magazine described me as Ralph Nader with cleavage!

> It was my identification with the victims that helped me understand why in my own life for such a long time it had been so difficult to ever get anyone to listen to me *about anything*.

Admittedly, these days I'm a far cry from the poor, scattered Erin Brockovich you meet at the beginning of the movie. I refer to "her" in the third person now because, for all intents and purposes, that Erin, overwhelmed with the chores of everyday living, is a dead and buried relic of my past. It took me a long time to overcome the many major obstacles that stood between me and success. These were obstacles set in place long before I'd ever heard of PG&E, before I'd had my first child, before I'd even started high school—obstacles that blocked the key to my self-discovery by keeping a padlock on my soul.

To begin with, I was born dyslexic. This condition caused everyone to misjudge my behavior from the time I was a child, to label me as "different" or "difficult," or as "a slow learner." It's surely one of the reasons I felt early on I was being bottled with a warning label, placed on a high shelf, and kept out of easy reach.

> I was born dyslexic.

I knew I wasn't dumb, even if everyone else thought I was. Overcoming my dyslexia became the first serious obstacle in my life, the first challenge that led me to discover the power and focus of my inner strength.

And so it is that these days, everywhere I go, when people ask me the same question—"Erin, how did you do it?"—they don't have an inkling about what they are really asking. I know they think they mean, How did I help win the case?, but what they're seeking is the answer to a much deeper and more complex question. The answer to how I helped defeat PG&E really answers all these questions: How did I change my life? How did I rescue myself from the oblivion it seemed I was so surely headed for? Where did I get the strength to keep pushing forward against the enormous challenges that stood in the way of my own success? How did I overcome the burdens of dyslexia, single motherhood, poverty, and loneliness? And finally, how did I find the inner strength to move the mountains of self-imposed obstacles in my journey toward becoming the me I always knew I could be?

How indeed?

The answers are a whole other story that starts when I was just a little girl growing up in Kansas, about to take the first steps of what would prove my long, difficult, and ultimately rewarding journey on the road to self-discovery, inner knowledge, and emotional empowerment.

What follows, then, is not just the story of *what* I did in my life, *but how I did it.*

CHAPTER TWO

Conversations with Myself

I was fortunate to grow up in Lawrence, Kansas, a part of America's heartland, in a household with wonderful parents who had strong, deeply ingrained values regarding family, land, and health. Their marriage was actually quite progressive, ahead of the social and economic curve. For example, as far back as I can remember, they both always worked outside the home. My dad was an engineer, my mother a journalist. This made them equal partners in their marriage at a time when most women were taught by their parents that marriage meant staying home, having babies, making dinner, and cleaning house.

They cherished me unconditionally from the day I was born, and they worked to instill their moral values in me, values based on a solid foundation of personal integrity. Respect for family was everything. My two older brothers, Tommy and Frankie, my older sister Jodie, and I were all taught this same doctrine, regardless of our gender or age. And although we had no strong religious upbringing, there was a very strong sense of what I like to call *good karma* in our home, a reflection of the spiritual policies that our parents instilled in us.

One of these policies was based on my parents' shared belief that the worst thing any of us could ever do in life was to tell a lie.

> There was a very strong sense of what I like to call good karma in our home, a reflection of the spiritual policies that our parents instilled in us.

Out of this came certain family rules that no one ever broke. For us children, lying to our parents was about the single worst thing we could do. We were taught that persistence and drive, rather than deception and falsehoods, were the best tools, the only ones really, that could get us through the obstacles life would throw in our way.

My parents were unwavering in their support—on a good day, a bad day, a day of outright crisis, it didn't matter. They were a constant, and they taught by setting their own example rather than preaching their message. Looking back, I realize now that I not only didn't fully understand the great gift of this solid moral foundation but as a teenager I actually rebelled against it. I thought the beat of the drummer I wanted to march to was keeping a different set of rhythms. Because of it, I found myself for many years wandering aimlessly through the desert of my life, even though the moral and spiritual roots of all that I would eventually draw upon to take on Hinkley had already been firmly established in me while I was still a child.

*   *   *

We all have ideas of how things should and shouldn't be. The one thing I can recall hearing as a child and the one thing that I have tried to pass on to my own children is what that old cliché says: "Don't judge a book by its cover." Although we should all know better, it is exactly what we continue to do. I experienced the damage of this type of thinking all the way back in elementary school, and for years after, until I was finally and officially diagnosed as being dyslexic. Before then, I was constantly being labeled by everyone—teachers, friends, and schoolmates alike— as "pretty but dumb." The simple truth was, I couldn't learn the way society said I had to, and society was unwilling to concede that there was more than one way to teach and be taught. *"She's stupid . . ."* There was no willingness on anybody's part to give me credit for being a good person or to bother to look for any other possible answers as to why I wasn't like everyone else.

It wasn't until I reached high school and met a teacher by the name of Kathy Borseath that things finally began to change for me. Ms. Borseath marked a major turning point in my life when, after observing both the limits of my abilities and the range of my behavior, as they appeared to her, she realized that I *was* able to learn everything in class, but whenever I took a written test, I still failed. She knew something was wrong, but unlike everyone else in my life until then (except my parents), she didn't immediately dismiss me as a hopeless case. She gave me the chance to take my exams orally, which I did, and I passed every one.

This was the first time anyone considered the possibility I wasn't as stupid as everyone—including me—thought. Through Kathy Borseath's efforts, I made the first solid inroad on the pathway to the core of my inner strength. It had taken the kindness and extra effort of a teacher who believed in me, who could see through and beyond the scattered surface, what everyone else thought was the sum of what there was, to the value that was inside of me. It was really due to her that in 1978 I managed to graduate from high school, after which I enrolled at my hometown college, Kansas State University.

> The paths to inner strength, spiritual awakening, and intellectual learning aren't always straight and unbroken.

Unfortunately, for me and I think a lot of people, the paths to inner strength, spiritual awakening, and intellectual learning aren't always straight and unbroken. They're more like Dorothy's yellow brick road, filled with twists and turns and diversions that keep us from, rather than delivering us to, our intended goals. During my freshman year, those diversions piled up fast and furiously.

Cut loose from the normal restrictions of living at home, and being tall, blonde, eighteen, and popular, without a Kathy Borseath to help encourage and guide me, I soon reverted to my old, compensating-for-my-fears-of-inferiority ways. I'm sure it was because I was so afraid of failing that I put aside the books and instead successfully partied my way right out the school door. At least that way I had a good excuse for not making the grade. Instead, I majored in socializing to the point where my dorm mate used to chuckle that until she met me, she didn't think any single girl could stand out among 20,000 students all eager to get noticed.

Well, if anyone could, it was me. I loved to party until the wee hours, sleep until four the next day, skip all my classes, and start all over again as soon as the sun went down. It was a great lifestyle, or so I thought at the time. In reality, it was one of those poppy fields that distracted Dorothy on the road to Oz. My ongoing party came to a swift dead end when Dad received my first report card. He put his foot down and said, "No more." I begged him to let me continue, but he wouldn't budge.

Finally, after much pleading, I was allowed to transfer to Wade Business College, a private merchandising institution in Dallas, to study the business end of fashion and interior design, and then only because my brother Tommy was living and working there and promised Dad he'd keep a watchful eye on me. I vowed to my parents that this time I would seriously apply myself to my studies and try to learn enough to eventually be able to go into business, maybe even open my own retail establishment. I really tried to apply myself this time around, but I was discouraged by the same old learning difficulties, and so, to protect myself, I continued to remain focused on my two favorite subjects, good times and hot guys.

This was 1980, and the TV show *Dallas* was all the rage. Because of it, the city was *hopping*. I had just turned nineteen, was out on my own, and during my first semester I fell in with a bunch of coed party animals.

Sure enough, I quickly ran into academic trouble. I was constantly being kicked out of classes. One time I was suspended for three days for not wearing a bra (I didn't have an ample bod at the time so I didn't see the need for one). Another time I was tossed for three more days for not wearing pantyhose. Well, I *hated* pantyhose, and I couldn't understand why I had to wear them.

Somehow I managed to get through the two-year program in 19 months by attending summer sessions, during which time I earned extra spending money working at odd jobs. One of these was selling memberships at a health club, and that's when I discovered a new talent I didn't know I had. I was actually pretty good at it! People naturally took to me and always seemed interested in hearing what I had to say. I also worked in a men's retail clothing place, Danny's Menswear I think it was called, and I was salesperson of the month, *every month*. Looking back, I can see now that I was good at these jobs because I *liked* what I was doing. It was what my dad always used to tell me. "If you do what you like," he'd say, "you'll succeed in life." I was just beginning to discover that these were words to live by.

On balance, I'd have to say that going to college was a good experience for me. I still was into living party-hearty, but I also had begun to apply my social skills to making money as well as to having a good time. In 1980, at the tender age of nineteen, I received an associate in applied arts degree in fashion merchandising and interior design.

The day I received my degree was an important one for me in more ways than one. Although it was an effort on my part, by completing my studies, I had proven to myself that Ms. Borseath had been right, that once I understood how to make my so-called shortcomings work for me, I was actually pretty good at learning. The difference now was that even though I didn't have her with me, I had taken her initial push and used it to propel myself even further, with my dad's always good advice echoing in my brain. Both in classes and at my various jobs, I had found something that interested me, that stimulated my abilities and made me *want* to do well. For me, graduating from Wade was the equivalent of finding my way out of that poppy field and back onto my own yellow brick road.

*   *   *

Shortly after graduation in the fall of 1980, I was offered a job at Neiman Marcus's flagship store in Dallas. I would have taken it except the highest they would go in starting salary was $9,000, and that didn't seem to me to be anywhere near enough money to live on. So I passed and instead took a position with the Kmart organization, where the starting salary was $22,000. As an added incentive, they offered to relocate me to Los Angeles. I'd never

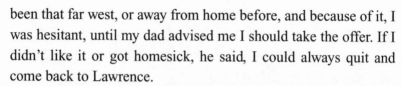

been that far west, or away from home before, and because of it, I was hesitant, until my dad advised me I should take the offer. If I didn't like it or got homesick, he said, I could always quit and come back to Lawrence.

I took his advice and accepted the job. I traveled out to L.A. with Lisa Runyon, a girlfriend and former roommate from Wade who was also hired by Kmart. She wound up working in Huntington Beach, while I was assigned to a store in Orange County. We quickly set up living quarters in the singles docking station they call Newport Beach. It was perfect! The best singles beach on the West Coast!

Unfortunately, from day 1, I wasn't into my job, and I stayed with it only three months before handing in my resignation. The day-to-day office chores didn't really suit me, like having to clean up after customers' kids who would make a complete mess in the bathroom. That didn't seem to me to be what I had gone to college to learn. And anyway, I was, at this point still much more into socializing than anything as trivial as pursuing a career.

Not long after I quit, I decided to live in California for good, moving in with Tommy, who was already living in L.A. His being there was the real reason my dad let me move to the coast, and he promised to keep an eye on both Lisa and me. Shortly after, she moved in with us. We all spent our first holiday season in California on the warm and sunny beach, opening presents and barbecuing. For Tommy and me, having grown up in landlocked Kansas where the winter snow was always a couple of feet deep, and for

Lisa, who grew up in Illinois, it felt like we were all celebrating Christmas in paradise.

Now that I was blissfully unemployed, I wanted to kick back and really enjoy this time, although there were moments when it was hard to get this message through to Tommy. For instance, one time he asked me to go to the corner Seven-Eleven to get cigarettes. I said sure. Thirty minutes later he came by my room and saw that I was still getting ready. "I can't believe you," he said. "You still haven't left yet? I could have been gone and come back ten times by now."

"Well then," I said, "you should have."

"What are you doing, Erin?" I was dawdling in front of the mirror, putting on my makeup.

"Getting cleaned up."

"Jesus, who are *you* trying to impress?"

I looked at him and said, quietly, "Myself."

That was true. There was no one around, no one I thought I would run into. It was daytime, and all the good-looking guys were still at work. I just wanted to look good for *me*. In those days, my physical appearance was not just important to me; it was *everything* to me. Looking back, I'm not surprised that I drifted into the world of professional beauty pageants. I did pretty well at them, too, making it as far as Miss Pacific Coast 1981. Unfortunately, I didn't find them very much fun, or interesting, or involving. It was a good thing to do, *once,* after which I quickly realized the whole pageant thing was about how you looked, who wore the prettiest gown, who had the prettiest face—everything but who you actually *were*. It was a message that helped open my eyes to the limitations I had imposed on myself by becoming so preoccupied with my physical appearance. Plus, I didn't like all that male-power-over-bikini-babe thing that came with the turf. When it came to looks, I'd always had the power. It felt to me as though every guy in the business thought it was his divine right to sleep with whatever contestant he chose. I felt taken advantage of and used for most of the time that I was doing pageants (not to mention meeting some of the cattiest girls who ever lived!).

So I got out of that field, and, at the age of twenty-one, found myself once more aimless and adrift in the land of my unfocused youth. I had no particular interest in anything, just waiting for a cool breeze to come by and blow me in some exciting new direction.

Somehow I managed to catch a wind and sailed into a new job with a very straightlaced engineering and construction company. I had no real preparation for the position, but I found the work fascinating and so much more rewarding than beauty pageants. I did so well there that I thought about following in my dad's footsteps and becoming an electrical design engineer. I liked the work and thought I was learning an awful lot until one day, a few months after I began, I was suddenly fired—let go by the same woman who had hired me. What had happened was that I had showed up for my initial job interview in a slinky white dress, and as she was walking me down the hall to meet my future boss, every male head had popped out of the partitioned cubicles. That's when she murmured to me, "I think it's probably a mistake, and I don't know why I'm doing it, but

I'm going to give you a shot." Who knows, maybe they were desperate for employees. Whatever the reason, I got hired.

And then fired.

Her concern proved prophetic; the guys in the office liked me and I liked them, probably a little too much. Despite my good intentions (I'm sure my low-cut dresses didn't help), I still hadn't found a way to let people see who I really was and what I could actually do. My best personal asset—my just-another-pretty-face-and-figure inclination for having a good time—continued to be my worst professional qualification.

> Despite my good intentions (I'm sure my low-cut dresses didn't help), I still hadn't found a way to let people see who I really was and what I could actually do.

Still, even though I'd been fired, I felt the experience had been somehow positive because, if nothing else, it had opened my eyes to the fact that I actually did have a brain. If I had really wanted to, I then knew, I could have kept right up with the rest of this pack. This was a job in which even though the men still had their tongues out, I felt I could get above all that and apply my mind to my work. As a result, I was determined more than ever to find another job, in the same field if possible, and continue my professional development.

*   *   *

Not long after I was fired from the engineering company, I met Shawn Brown, a local house painter. We started seeing each other, and almost before we knew it, were going together. Things got serious, and we began making plans to get married. Looking back now, I know this wasn't something I did out of love, not even back then, but because I felt it was expected, not just of me, but of all young girls my age. It was what you were *supposed* to do. It's a very insidious hometown syndrome. I'd grown up with a group of girlfriends, and the values of my world revolved around them—Amy, Susan, Maylee, Shelley, Laurie, Brent, Janie, Lisa, Lynn, and Betty! Yah! We all hung out together with the baddest boys in town, and we loved to party! We were known as The Brew Crew! One by one they had all found guys and married them, and most were already having babies. I felt the pressure from being the lone single girl left, and I thought I was supposed to get married just like they had. When Shawn came along, I figured he'd be as good as anyone else for the job. I brought him home to Lawrence to meet my parents, and I broke the news of our engagement to them.

Surprise, surprise, they were less than overjoyed. Shawn was a house painter, and on top of that only twenty years old. *A younger man!* My parents had serious reservations about my getting married, but I was determined to go ahead.

We were married April 24, 1982, and by that September I was pregnant. When I found out I was expecting, I had to leave yet another job I had taken that I liked, this one at the Karl Menninger Institute in nearby Topeka. I was a secretary and was good at it. I had combined my social skills with the recent revelation that I actually was in possession of a working brain.

The job would have lasted except my pregnancy developed complications. I discovered I had a condition known as *placenta previa.* That's where the placenta lays on the bottom of the uterus rather than the top. Because of it, I was forced to spend most of my time in bed. I did nothing but eat for months. The night I gave birth to Matthew, I was so bored that I had actually gotten up, dressed, and went out to see a movie—*ET*—which proved to be a huge mistake. Before the little guy could even point his magic finger and say he wanted to go home, I had to be rushed to the hospital for an emergency C-section, complicated by a mild case of toxemia.

Even before I left the maternity ward, I fell into a serious postpartum depression. At the time of Matt's birth, I weighed in at a whopping 190 pounds. My mental situation then took another turn for the worse when, shortly after I found out we were moving to St. Louis because Shawn had been transferred again, I began to suspect that he was seeing someone else. All of my worlds were collapsing. I was the mother of a newborn baby, I was being forced to move away from my parents and all my friends, and although he swore he was not, I believed Shawn had lied about an affair. It was a tremendous blow to me, and as far as I was concerned, the end of us as a couple. Although for purely practical reasons we stayed together for a little while longer, I knew our marriage was over. He had compromised my ethics, my morals, and my spiritual values. From that moment on, I devoted all my married time to my baby.

*   *   *

In spite of my convictions and best intentions, before Shawn actually moved out of our house, I became pregnant again. Fifteen months after Matt had been born, I gave birth to Katie. She was an interesting child for me and posted a whole new series of complications in my life. First of all, she came along very quickly on the heels of Matt, and I wasn't quite prepared for this mother lode of responsibility. To make matters worse, my marriage, which was already a sham to me, became volatile at times. I could never forgive Shawn for lying to me. Forget about love, I just didn't *trust* him anymore.

Not long after Katie was born, we all moved again, this time to Lodi, California, where Shawn had taken a job with Naugles, a new food franchise. I felt adrift once more, this time in a meaningless sea of tacos!

Shawn was gone all the time, and I got so bored I'd find myself wandering over to the local Kmart to buy every power nozzle they had in stock. Then, while the kids napped, I'd test them all out on the front lawn, trying to find one strong enough to break down a black widow's handiwork. For your useless information file, Lodi has the biggest black widow spiders in the world.

And I felt like I was caught in its tightest web. We had a little duplex, no friends, and no outside interests. I developed a case of extreme anxiety and went through a series of quite severe panic attacks. I felt emotionally alone, out of love with my husband, and I missed my parents. And I was having a difficult time trying to raise two little children.

Just when I thought I was really going to lose it, Shawn was transferred yet again, this time to Reno, Nevada. I made up my mind I wasn't going to go with him, and I told him so. He was angry, and he accused me of abandoning him, but in the end he went to Reno and I went back home to my parents in Lawrence. I was determined to make a clean break, but, to my surprise, Mom and Dad convinced me for the sake of the children I should go back to my husband and try to make things work. If I did, they said, they would help us buy a home in Reno to help us finally settle down.

I reluctantly took their advice, but as I should have known, things didn't get any better between us—how could they—and I soon began looking for a new job. I found one at E.F. Hutton, which hired me to assist several of their brokers. I have always had a natural photographic mind—I can read a 500-page report, and after a single pass-through, I can point out all the inconsistencies. That skill was what got me the job, but because of my dyslexia, I started making silly but costly mistakes, like the time a client asked me to look up his account and tell him how much he had in it. I did and said the balance was $16,000, when in fact it was only $1,600.

The only reason I wasn't fired was because my immediate bosses liked me, including one by the name of Steve Brockovich.

Steve and I really hit it off. Shawn, meanwhile, was convinced that we were having an affair. Talk about projecting one's own guilt onto a partner. I finally agreed to see a marriage counselor with Shawn, but only because I thought that would be the best way to get the message across that our relationship was really and truly over. We went, and we didn't get anywhere. He just didn't want to hear what he didn't want to hear. In the spring of 1987, I finally made the big move on my own and filed suit for divorce.

A year and a half later, Steve left Hutton to take a vice president opening at Dean Witter Reynolds, and I went along with him. For the next two years I worked as his assistant, and eventually we began dating. In 1989, Steve became my second husband.

Even though he was supposedly out of the picture, my ex was hurt and angry, and he managed to convince himself that *I* was the one who had wronged *him,* and determined to make my life miserable. He started telephoning, supposedly to talk to me about how the children were, but really to verbally abuse me. During our conversations he'd suddenly start calling me various versions of "Brocka____" (just fill in your favorite derogatory word!). We had joint custody, and he used that to stir up more trouble. Either he wouldn't bring the kids home on time, or worse, without any regard for their feelings of disappointment, to mess me up, he'd simply "forget" to pick them up at all.

Steve, meanwhile, became increasingly frustrated with my ex's actions, particularly how, one way or another, he continued to try to insinuate himself into our life. And because Shawn never paid his child support, Steve had to support all of us. To try to get some money from my ex, I kept hauling him into court to make him pay his fair share.

It was a peculiar kind of hell that seemed never ending.

To help ease our financial burdens, I decided once again to go back to work. The only way I could do it was to ship my kids back to my parents in Kansas, which I reluctantly did. They weren't Steve's responsibility, they were mine, and I had no other choice but to entrust them to my folks until we were solidly back on our feet.

I found a job with Ron Garrett and Associates, an advertising agency that unexpectedly turned into one of the more pleasant experiences of my life. For the first time in a long time, I looked forward to getting up in the morning. I had a ball, laughing all day while being able to work with some very creative people. The only problem was, after spending eight or nine hours in a very heady atmosphere, I'd return home only to find an increasingly sullen husband. As it turned out, Steve didn't particularly like the reality of my sudden and new independence. He became angrier and angrier. He began to "moo" at me whenever I'd pass in front of him, his way of expressing dissatisfaction.

I could see much more clearly then that I had allowed Steve's dominating identity to submerge mine, to the point where my self-esteem, never that high, had hit a new all-time low. I needed a quick fix and came up with what I thought was the perfect solution. I decided the best way to boost my confidence would be to get my chest lifted with breast implants.

And believe me, *it worked!* Suddenly I began getting *much* more attention from men than I ever had before.

And then, as if on cue, I became pregnant.

Steve insisted he didn't want any more turmoil in his life. I didn't have the inner strength to resist him, and reluctantly I got an abortion. This was one of the most difficult decisions I had ever had to make. In the end I think I did it because I truly believed it would make things better between us.

I was wrong, of course. How could they, after something like that? Sure enough, everything got worse in every possible way. I developed another round of serious anxiety disorders, and this time they manifested themselves into a stubborn bout of anorexia.

I wound up committed to a hospital in Sparks, Nevada, for 14 days, as the doctors searched for an effective treatment to keep me from wasting away. One of the team that worked on me was a woman by the name of Mary Ann Potter, a double-mastectomy survivor and single mother of five. Mary Ann's own survival saga inspired me, and when I told her so, she put her hand on my shoulder and said that was very good. Then she vowed to help me survive as well, by leading me to the true path to find my way back—*to myself.*

After having been emotionally beaten down by two men, to the point where I was willing to abort my own unborn child, I had somehow managed to find a woman dedicated to saving the living and breathing soul that was still alive inside of me.

Mary Ann Potter often sat with me, trying to get me to

remember how well liked I had been in high school and college, and how much my family—my *real* family, my mom and dad who had raised me, as opposed to the men I had married—truly loved me for *me*. Not just for my looks but for my spirit and warmth and the essence that was my soul.

She then did something I'll never forget. She asked me to go to my room and talk everything out with myself, *to* myself, as a way of closing this chapter of my life and moving on.

It was a brilliant notion, and one that I highly recommend to everyone. It is the best way I've ever found of giving a voice to my inner self. I talked to *me* in my room out loud for the rest of the day and deep into the night. I discovered that talking to myself was a great way of letting things out, of putting a voice to exactly what it was I was feeling inside. Even though the movies like to teach us that people who talk to themselves are crazy, I stand as living proof that people who talk to themselves are actually quite sane! It is a great thrill to find someone who really cares about you and is willing to hear everything you have to say.

> People who talk to themselves are actually quite sane!

One thing you discover when you have a conversation with yourself is that you don't have to ask a friend, you don't have to ask a lawyer, you don't have to ask your local guru, you don't have to ask *anybody* for advice. Because, as you quickly discover, you already know the answers to all the questions you have. You just have to give yourself a chance to *listen,* to *hear,* to *consider,* and to *respond.*

A good way to begin talking to yourself is to start by simply asking, out loud, looking into a mirror if possible, "What is really important here?" Then, again, out loud, tell yourself all the responses you are thinking.

Take a moment right now to consider how many talk shows there are on TV today, how many "experts" get paid the big bucks for what we think is their wisdom, their insight into *our* lives.

> **You are your inner strength.**

Now I ask you, how can they really know what is going on inside of you? *You are the only person who knows yourself. You are the only person who knows what is right for you!* You *are* your inner strength.

Listen to the echoes that are the voice of your own emotions, and you'll find the answers to all your questions coming back out to you from the inside.

One thing to remember, and this is crucial, is that if you're going to talk to yourself, you have to be ready for a healthy dose of *honesty* because if you're really ready to look into that mirror, you won't be able to lie to that person on the other side of the glass. *He or she will know it.*

It's really not that difficult. Which one of us can look at ourselves and honestly say we have not done something in our lives to be ashamed of? What's important to remember here is shame is not the operating factor. *Honesty* is. That first night, when I finished giving myself a good talking to, and listened hard to every word I had to say, I was ready to do what Dr. Potter said I would, say goodbye to what was about to become my dead and buried past.

Trust me. Try it. It works.

*   *   *

So I said goodbye to a past that ex #2 was very much a part of. I think he believed that my confinement meant I was a mental case and that it stigmatized him in the professional community. I believe this was the moment my marriage came to an end. He now viewed me as a defective wife.

Hey, dude, as far as I was concerned, that was just fine. In 1990 we agreed to get divorced. I have to tell you, the night I signed my papers I went to the mirror, smiled, and congratulated myself out loud!

However, as I discovered in the following weeks and months, even though I had been able to do what I intended, and believed I was right, there was still some residue of tangible fear lingering inside of me. What was I afraid of? One night I asked myself that question out loud, and I immediately came up with the answer. Most of all I was afraid of being lonely again, of being without a male companion. That I might go two months, hell, two *years* with no sex!

Now, don't get me wrong. I admire people who can make a commitment and stick to it. And I *like* the idea of having a partner

> Most of all I was afraid of being lonely again, of being without a male companion.

I can share my life with. Yet, here I was, twenty-nine years old, divorced twice, and utterly alone. It wasn't hard for me to understand why I was scared. Of course, talking to myself was what got me through this, and a little episode confirmed to me the rightness of my methods. One night I confided my feelings to a girl-friend, who, frankly, didn't have a clue as to what I was really trying to say. "Oh," she chuckled, "I know what it is," she suddenly said. "Go out and buy yourself a vibrator and you'll be fine!"

That little quip made me sit right down and give myself a quick fix-me-up oral exam. I only had one question to ask myself this time: Why didn't I just stick to talking to myself?

In the days and months that followed the split, the physical distance I put between myself and Steve underscored how emotionally far apart we had actually become during our marriage. I was once more spiritually isolated, surviving alone with my two kids, with no money, no child support from ex #1, no direction in my life, a screwed-up past, and an unknown future. And all men seemed to care about was my new improved cup size. For the first time, this didn't seem to me like caring at all. Just the opposite, in fact. Ironically, by getting my implants, I had gained a new insight to my own, real worth, or at the time, the lack of it I was feeling. At least I knew then that my new breasts were not going to be the beginning and the end of my existence.

I had made some major emotional leaps, but I knew I was still a long way from completing the journey I had begun, with Dr. Potter's guidance, down the road to self-discovery, self-realization, and self-confidence.

> For the first time, this didn't seem to me like caring at all.

*   *   *

I was making real progress. I still cared how others regarded me, I still wanted to be loved, but now, even more important, I also wanted to be *liked*. I decided I needed some comfort time with the two people I knew I could count on to always be there for me, *unconditionally*. My parents, bless them, invited me to once more come back to Lawrence, Kansas, where they promised they would help me put the pieces of my life back together.

And then a very strange thing happened.

All the work I had done with Dr. Potter, all the talking to myself and rebuilding of my self-esteem made me doubt not just the wisdom of going home again but whether or

> I still wanted to be loved, but now, even more important, I also wanted to be liked.

not going home was such a good idea after all. I began to see a pattern to my behavior, that I ran home to mommy and daddy each time I experienced something traumatic in my life. The more I thought about it, the further back I was able to go, until I suddenly remembered the first time I had done this. It was an incident from my childhood that I had kept repressed for all these years. I was in the second grade, when one day after school I went over to my girlfriend's house, and her father sexually abused me. I don't remember many of the actual details, but I do remember how, afterward, all I had wanted to do was go home. This episode became a primal event that had helped shape a fight-or-flight pattern of behavior in me. Any time anything went wrong in my adult life, as in each of the failures of my two marriages, I somehow linked those traumas to that one and repeated my childhood response by running home like a little girl to mommy and daddy's big protective arms.

Despite these doubts, I knew I needed to regroup and refocus. And so it was in that frame of mind I made the long drive home from my dinky little apartment in Reno where Matt, Katie, and I had been living during my divorce. Before it was over, however, this trip would turn into a nightmare. It was as if the gods were trying to warn me about the very wrong turn I was about to take.

I put everything in storage except our summer clothes, put the kids and their pet rabbit, Thumper, into the car, and took off for Lawrence. I remember pulling out of Reno and hearing Sinead O'Connor's song come on the radio, "Nothing Compares 2 U." I was surprised by how much it moved me. Despite everything that had gone down, I realized at that moment there was a part of me that still felt something deeply for Steve. It was then that I measured all the frustration and misery of our relationship alongside some of the best times I had ever had with a man. Before I knew it, I began sobbing, knowing I had failed again, my twice-divorced tail dragging heavily between my pretty long legs.

I'm certain now it was the distraction of that sudden emotional upset that caused me to miss the obvious physical signs warning of the danger up ahead. Because it was early spring, I figured the weather was warm enough to allow me to take the more direct northern route back to Lawrence. Although by now the sky had turned a combination soft pale and dark gray, I still didn't realize I was driving straight into a late-season Plains blizzard in the making.

Or maybe didn't want to. I was determined to make this trip, to get back to the safety and security of my family, to prove that I could handle caring for my own children no matter what. What I didn't know was the extent of the next "no matter what."

I drove all day, checked into a Motel Six in Elko, Nevada, put the kids to bed, and for the first time felt a real sense of foreboding start to creep over me. The next morning I awakened to high winds, black skies, and horrific rains. The day before it had been in the 80s, now it was barely 40. Just before we hit the road, I heard a voice on the radio say there was a possibility the I-70 might have to be closed down. I decided to play it safe. I called my dad. I wanted him to have my license plate number, as a caution flag, just in case.

Sure enough, by the time I hit Wyoming, the snow was coming down so hard, thick, and wet I actually got the sensation I was driving backward as I tried to plow through the total whiteout. At one point I tried to slip behind a convoy of big, protective trucks, but I lost them and control of my car on a curve that sent the kids and me smack into the middle of a huge snowdrift.

So here we were, stuck on the highway, half-buried in snow with nothing but our summer clothes and that rabbit. It was scary and off-balancing. I had no way of keeping us warm. I didn't want to keep the car engine running for heat because I was worried about exhaust fumes. The winds kept howling, the kids were terrified, and I had this awful, inescapable feeling that we were all going to die in this prairie snowstorm!

After a while Matt wondered aloud what we were going to do for food. That's when I turned, looked at him, and broke out laughing at the utter absurdity of the whole situation. "Well," I said, "there's always Thumper."

*   *   *

Finally, after what seemed like an eternity, I saw a car coming up through the blurry distance. As I was soon to find out, when my dad hadn't heard anything from me, he had called the highway patrol. The policemen used their car to pull us out of the snow and put us back on the road. They then escorted us to the nearest hotel where the kids and me (and even Thumper) all collapsed into much-needed sleep.

The next day the storm had ended, and feeling lucky to be alive, I put the kids and ol' Thump back into the car, and we drove nonstop all the way to Lawrence. As you can well imagine, everyone was glad to see us, grateful we had made it alive and in one piece.

However, the image of pushing against the storm continued to stay with me, and I wasn't sure why until I realized that what had taken place on the highway had provided an important lesson about the nature of self-determination. In a very real sense I had done something crucial to my survival. In another sense, I had put into physical action one of the notions my father had always taught me about life. No matter how severe the storm that's trying to blow you off the road, the important thing is to keep pushing and never give up. I had made it through the storm on the highway; I could make it through the other storms in my life. It was one of life's lessons I had learned the hard way, but one that had been well worth it. That day I gained a new perspective about the nature of life, about what was really important and what wasn't, and how to survive it all.

> No matter how severe the storm that's trying to blow you off the road, the important thing is to keep pushing and never give up.

*   *   *

After surviving the snowstorm on the interstate, my emotional differences with Steve seemed, by comparison, quite petty, and my choices crystal clear. I remembered what I had felt when that song had come on, and I knew I wanted to see him again. I was able to admit to myself that, yes, I did miss some really good things about Steve, and I was sure we could work everything out. I'd get a job in Reno, the kids would come and live with us, and everything would be all right again.

Or so I thought.

Or so I hoped.

When I got back to Reno, Steve was indeed as happy to see me as I was him, and we started seeing each other again. That first night we made love and everything seemed idyllic. However, after a few weeks, reality set in and just as before, we both realized it just wasn't going to work. That July my mother came for a visit, and she noticed that I was looking run down. The sparkle had once more faded from my eyes.

The next day, without anyone knowing, I went to the drugstore and bought an EPT—or home pregnancy test. It took exactly 10 seconds to turn positive. Oh my God, I thought, was I pregnant *again?* How could this have happened? Well, I knew how. The real question was why. I told my mother, and she was as surprised and disappointed as I was. The only realistic solution, I immediately thought, was to get rid of it. By now, my emotions were spilling into each other like the ingredients of a margarita in a blender. Here I was, about to have another child.

What was worse, this time not just Steve but *everyone* wanted me to get an abortion! I kept hearing this unified chorus of opinion from my family and friends—"You're not married. How can you do this to yourself . . ." and so on. It continued all day and night, everywhere I turned.

To be honest, there was a part of me that agreed with them, that felt they were right, that I should not, under any circumstances, have this baby. However, there was another, stronger part of me that wouldn't hear of it. There was a new, innocent life in my belly, and . . . *I wanted to keep it.*

My OB/GYN was the only person who thought I was doing the right thing. He was not in favor of this abortion. For one thing, he wasn't sure how far along I was. He suggested I have a sonogram, which I did, and the results revealed something truly amazing to me. I was due to give birth on July 12. The date was startling, although at first I couldn't figure out why. He checked my chart, and we discovered that that was the exact date one year earlier that I had had my abortion.

Whoaa!

That coincidence had quite an impact. I realized right then I had somehow been given a second chance to have this baby! It had come back to me one more time and wanted so desperately to come out, as if it were more than another life, as if it were the very spirit of my inner soul. It too was undergoing an incubation, and had sent me a special delivery that I knew I could not turn away from.

That's when I finally decided once and for all, no matter what, I was going to have it. And I wasn't going to look to Steve for anything. I wouldn't stay in town and "haunt" him with his child. Instead, I would bring my new baby into the world, take the other kids, and move on with our lives. If Steve chose to honor his obligation to pay child support, *the right thing to do,* that would be great. If not, I'd just have to find another way to get through that hurricane as well.

*   *   *

Steve insisted I take a paternity test before he would accept that the child I was carrying was his. As luck would have it, I had fallen short of a little-known law that says that from the date of a divorce, for 45 days, if there is a pregnancy, it cannot be contested. Guess what, I fell 2 days short!

Steve, of course, had convinced himself I must have slept with someone else while we had been separated. I told him he was wrong, but that didn't matter. Nor did the results of the blood test, which came back 99.9999 percent proving his paternity. There was no question to anybody but him that the baby was his.

I took the kids and moved into a small apartment in Reno. I figured since I chose to have my baby, I had also chosen the responsibility of taking care of it.

As for Steve, all I can say about how I felt toward him is contained in one of my favorite movie lines of all time. There is a scene at the end of *Indiana Jones and the Last Crusade* when they find the Holy Grail and suddenly the evil, greedy Nazi comes in and, seeking the right vessel among many, is instructed, "Choose wisely." Then, of course, he very confidently makes the wrong choice and loses his own life.

> *Choose wisely.*

Choose wisely.
Very good advice.

* * *

As soon as Matt and Katie started school that fall, I got a part-time job to pay the bills. I may have been free, but I was also broke, weak, and haunted by my old fears of loneliness. I was also determined that my children were going to have a decent holiday. I waited until after midnight on Christmas Eve to buy a tree for $5. That's how pathetic things had gotten. I didn't even have enough money to fill stockings. After I put them to bed, I stayed up all night crying so hard from the pain of my loneliness that the whole bed shook.

* * *

Just before dawn, after I had cried myself out, I decided to stop feeling so bad. I started talking to myself again, confiding in the best and most trusted listener I knew, my only true friend. "What's the matter with you, Erin," I said. "Can't you think about anyone else but yourself? You have two beautiful children who need all the loving and caring you can give them. If you're not going to be there for them, who will? Come on, Erin . . ."

I was getting better at these conversations, both on the talking and listening end. The more chaos that came at me, the more I would go into myself for stability, wisdom, and serenity. I think part of it was all the practice, but it was also partly the fact that I was dyslexic, which pushed my learning curve in a different direction. I was like a blind person whose sense of hearing was sharper. Talking to myself was my compensation for not being able to learn immediately from my own experiences as they happened.

I talked to myself every night between Christmas and New Year's, and I was able to get through this latest bout of depression by working on it from the inside out. My survival instinct kicked into overtime, and with the coming new year, I was determined to refocus all of my energies on getting myself together. I felt renewed, reenergized, as though I was traveling down a different road, when suddenly, out of nowhere, I was literally sideswiped in my car at an intersection, an accident that sent me spinning into what would eventually prove to be the most important turning point of my life.

I was rushed to a nearby hospital emergency room where the doctors on duty didn't discover the tiny fact that I had suffered a C5/C6 herniation of my spinal cord. Because I was pregnant, they had decided not to administer an MRI or take any x-rays. As a result of the injury, almost immediately my body started to deteriorate. I became dizzy, and I could barely stand up. I felt like there was a knife sticking through the back of my shoulder blades, and no one had a clue as to why.

And then, on top of everything else, Katie fell deathly ill. She ran a fever that spiked to 106. I rushed her to the hospital, carrying her in my arms with Matthew hanging on my legs in the middle of a blizzard. The doctors diagnosed her as having come down with a strep infection that had broken loose into her bloodstream. The hospital had to work against a staggering deadline to bring her temperature down before it fried her brain. They packed her in ice and hooked her up to what looked like a million IVs. It was touch and go for a while, but eventually her fever broke and she recovered.

It was a rough couple of days, but in a strange way a positive experience because it helped me refocus my priorities on something other than my own physical ailments. I had no one else to care for my children, and I was determined not just to be a good mother to my two kids (and my third on the way) but the best damn mother who ever lived.

In April 1991, my beautiful baby, Elizabeth, was born, and while I loved and adored her, the physical load was just too much for me. I was in constant pain from the automobile accident, and the relentlessness of single motherhood was starting to take its toll. For my own sanity, I knew I needed a break from Reno. Which is why, when a girlfriend asked me if I wanted to go to L.A. with her, I jumped at the chance. My parents happily agreed to watch the kids, knowing I was more than overdue for a little break for some much needed R&R.

It was on this trip that I first met the biker, and my life took another wildly unexpected turn, one that would have long-lasting consequences I never would have dreamed possible.

PART TWO

. . . .

How I Did It

CHAPTER THREE

You Do It Because You Have To!

I was finally having some fun! I was looking good, and because I was no longer pregnant, I was able to drink again. Alcohol not only helped ease the constant pain I was in from my accident but it also, let's face it, made life a little more fun.

One night my girlfriend and I were at the Sagebrush Cantina, a local hangout in Calabasas, California, where we went at night and where two minutes didn't pass before every guy in the place would be all over us. Here I was, this seemingly beautiful blonde, perfect in every way, at least in their fantasies, until they found out I had a couple of kids back at the corral. That bit of info always stopped them dead in their hot little tracks as effectively as if I were holding up a giant cross in front of a pack of single-but-looking vampires.

On one night I happened to catch this fellow's eyes and watched as he maneuvered his way from table to table, until he was right on top of us. Here comes another one, I thought to myself, all cocky and confident, complete with a beach-bum ponytail and all the silver bracelets his arms could hold. He said his name was Jorge, and he was, as I quickly found out, a natural shooter of all things bull. He sat right down and started telling us all about his Harley, a smooth line of fire until he interrupted himself with a smirk on his face as he looked into my eyes and said, "I'll bet you're a graduate of Pepperdine."

I smirked right back at him and replied, "No, Harvard."

"Oh," he said, and for the first time looked a little thrown. "I'm so sorry . . ."

I said nothing. By this time, as you might imagine, I had more than a little chip on my shoulder when it came to men, especially the good-looking kind with the king-sized broom they liked to use to sweep me off my feet.

It didn't seem to bother him, though. He asked me if I'd like to hang with him the rest of the night. That's when I let him have the other barrel. "Oh, I'm so sorry, I won't be able to. I have two children at home and a six-week-old baby with a diaper filled with poo-poo that needs changing."

What do you know, his high-horse never even so much as whinnied. "You have a baby," he said. "That's cool. So do I." With that, he took out a photo of his little girl, showed it to me, and started telling me all about her.

What can I say? *He got me.*

Looking back, I learned a valuable lesson that night. Jorge may have been a lot of things, but one thing he wasn't was easily thrown. He had a manner about him that was charming, seductive even, but the key to it wasn't his good looks, his biker jewelry, or any of that. It was his way of treating people, women especially, the same exact way he wanted to be treated. He didn't condescend, he didn't come on hot and heavy, and he didn't put on a fancy show filled with sliding two-steps and self-promotion. He let his manner speak for itself, to show the way he was, as he was, and in return he expected people to not just accept him but to return his courtesy by according him the same. In presentation at least, he was a living, breathing version of the Golden Rule my father had always insisted his children follow: *Do unto others as you would have others do unto you.*

Jorge and I started dating, and I have to say he seemed like a lot of fun, and fun, as I say, was something I hadn't had in quite a while. Moreover, he wasn't afraid of me, he had a child of his own, and just as important, he *liked* children!

Things were going fine. I returned to Reno to get the kids, and in the meantime, he found a little apartment for me in Moorpark, Los Angeles (the "valley," as it's known), then came to Reno to get us. He packed up my little apartment, put us in a U-Haul, and drove us back out to L.A.

During the trip I was bouncing all over, and because of my untreated herniated disc, I was in severe agony. Jorge asked what the matter was, and I told him about my accident, adding that my attorney had done very little for me in the year and a half since it had happened. He said he knew some people who could help and as soon as we were settled, he'd get on it.

*　　*　　*

As excited as I was about actually moving back to L.A., my heart sank when I saw the apartment he had found. It was smack in the middle of a crack house! I lived there for exactly one hour. Two o'clock that morning I put my things and the kids back into the U-Haul and drove around until the middle of the next day, when I finally found a little house for rent in Northridge, California. It was a cockroach-infested, lead-paint-peeling-off-the-walls slum shack, but *it was available and I needed it.*

Not long after I moved in, Jorge said he knew a real lawyer I should talk to, Jim Vititoe, a fellow who had represented him in some lawsuit. I met with him, and he took my case. The first thing he did was get the other side's insurance company to finally fix my car, which had been wrecked in the crash and unusable ever since. I didn't want another car or a new one; I wanted mine back, all $6,500 worth of repairs notwithstanding. Jim then introduced me to a doctor by the name of Alvin Turken to see what could be done about my injuries.

I needed surgery on my neck, pretty dicey surgery at that, and it freaked me out. My mom and dad came to L.A. to help out, and before I knew it, the day had come when I found myself being wheeled into the operating room. Jim Vititoe came to the hospital with me, basically to hold my hand. Just before I was put under, I asked Dr. Turken if I was going to die.

"No," he said. "If that happened, how would I get paid?"

That made me laugh, and I calmed down a bit. Then I said, "What if I'm paralyzed from the surgery?"

"I'll tell you what," he said. "When you wake up, swing your ankles. If they move, you're not paralyzed." It was the last thing I heard before going under.

The surgery lasted nine hours, during which I bled profusely. The first thing I remember is waking up in the recovery room and hearing all the nurses laughing. Even before I was fully awake, I'd been twirling my ankles like plastic pinwheels on the Fourth of July! The miracle of it all is that I made a total recovery, with no loss of motion or range. All I have left is one gigantic scar down the front of my throat to remind me of how lucky I really am. I'll take it!

*   *   *

Meanwhile, my dad got to know Jorge and decided he didn't like him. He didn't buy the "sell" of Jorge's self, and he warned me against becoming too involved with him. At the same time, ex #2, who had remarried, decided in January 1992 that he was entitled to visitation rights to Beth, who had just turned nine months old. I couldn't believe this! He had been all but invisible during her birth and for most of the first year of her life, and then he had gone off and gotten married, and now, suddenly, he wanted a piece of her!

I decided to fight him because I feared this was only the first move in what had to be a plan on his part to get permanent and total custody of Beth. After all, he was married, I wasn't; he was doing well, I was in a neck brace. I went to Jim Vititoe for help, and he introduced me to his partner at the law firm, Ed Masry. Ed got me a heavy-hitting domestic attorney. The trial was brutal and nasty—a knock-down, drag-out custody battle. In the middle of all this, I got a phone call from my mother telling me that my older brother Tommy had suddenly and unexpectedly died.

*   *   *

I was devastated. I dropped the phone, screamed in disbelieving shock, and fell to the floor in a defeated heap. Tommy and I had always been close. He was 6 years older than I am, while my other brother, Frankie, is 13 years my senior and my older sister Jodie, 10. By the time I was five years old, both Frankie and Jodie were gone from the house, so for most of my childhood, it was only Tommy and me, and we did everything together. He had always been sickly and had suffered from asthma, and I remember my mom having to stay up late into the night to care for him during his attacks. Now he was gone forever.

He was only thirty-eight when it happened, so enthusiastic about life and so beautiful. He had been on a camping trip with some friends, and he unexpectedly went into anaphylactic shock and died. The weird thing about it was that there wasn't a single mark on his body, meaning that it didn't happen from a bee sting, which is the most common cause of this type of reaction. He probably ate something that he was allergic to, or he just breathed something in the air that proved toxic to his system.

His death profoundly changed everything inside of me. It awakened all the deadened values that I had grown up with and had somehow managed to displace during all these years of aimlessly pinballing through my own youth. I remember being at his funeral, and his body on display in an open casket. I was sitting in the front row shaking so badly I thought every limb in my body was going to fall off. All of a sudden I felt my dad's shoulder on my right side, and my brother Frankie's on my left. I told my dad I didn't think I could go through this. In response, he put one of his big hands on my knee to stop it from shaking and said, softly, "Look at me."

I did, and very firmly he said, "*You have to!*"

You have to.

Those words have stayed with me until this very day. Their stoicism, their strength, their fortitude, their *conviction*. They entered my soul like a search-and-save mission and resuscitated all that I had learned as a little girl from my mom and dad about the meaning and the value of life.

You *have* to.

> You have to. There are some things you just have to do. There is no choice, there is no decision, there is

There are some things you just have to do. There is no choice, there is no decision, there is no avoidance. Life is filled with certain obligations and responsibilities, but none more basic, primal, or important than the responsibilities we have to *ourselves.* I realized that up until that day I had been continually letting myself down. I had squandered so much energy, I had looked away rather than inside, I had ignored my inner strength rather than calling upon it. I had been living my life as if I were my car, blindsided by events that hurt me rather than helped me. I may have been behind the steering wheel, but I was not in control of what I never saw coming and even if I did wouldn't know how to avoid.

You have to.

That was the mindset that had been missing for me. The knowledge, the *belief,* that I actually had the ability to control my own destiny, as long as I recognized there were some things that *had* to be done along the way.

You have to.

I remember staring at my dad after those words came out, realizing how strong, how secure, how *right* he was. It was then, through his simple words and loving touch, that I managed to turn the tragedy of Tommy's death into the moment of my own emotional and spiritual rebirth.

Just before leaving L.A. for Lawrence, where the funeral was, I'd called Steve to tell him I was going to have to miss the court date, and I was greatly surprised by his reaction when he said he felt really bad about Tommy. Now, upon my return, I discovered he had dropped all his lawsuits, and not long after, for the first time he began paying child support.

*   *   *

That summer, I went to trial against the driver who had hit me. I was well prepared to testify, and the firm was confident of our chances for victory.

So, of course, what happened? We lost, and badly.

It was a disaster for me. I had hoped a decent settlement would enable me to pay back my parents some of the money they had laid out since the accident and help me get back on my own two feet. We wound up settling for a pittance. After legal fees and medical expenses, I wound up with just under $5,000, which I handed over to my dad, leaving the kids and me with exactly nothing.

First chance I got, I had lunch with Jim Vititoe, and I vented all my frustrations on him, blaming the firm for what I really couldn't face, the reality of my own failures, and then I added for the hell of it, how bad he was at returning phone calls. Then it hit me. "You know what?" I said, out of the nowhere that was then everywhere for me. "You need someone to do exactly that. How about if you hired me to answer your phones?"

He said no immediately, of course, but I refused to accept that answer. I kept at it the whole day. I was relentless! Then I called him the next day and worked on him some more. He finally called me in to the office to talk it over with Ed Masry. At one point Ed turned to him and said, "What are we going to hire her for? Other than sit up by herself, what can she do?"

I was so offended by that! He was talking as if I weren't even in the room. "Hey, asshole," I said. True, I had showed up in boots and a short skirt, and my big boobs pressing against my low-cut blouse, but still, I thought I deserved *some* kind of respect. This was the way I liked to dress. It wasn't meant to impress or offend. It wasn't premeditated, and certainly it wasn't meant to anger anyone to the point of insult and ridicule. It was something I like to call "individualism." If I dressed a different way, would it make me any smarter?

If for no other reason than I had impressed them with my persistence, they finally broke down and gave me a job. Ed gets a lot of Brownie points for having a strong-enough sense of self to not be afraid to admit that maybe some "big-mouthed, big-breasted chick" might actually know how to *do* something.

I was really excited about this opportunity. I couldn't wait to tell my dad that I had gotten a real job that was going to pay me $1,200 a month.

I started Labor Day weekend, September 1991. The backlog of calls was so heavy that I started returning some myself, and I quickly discovered that the firm's clients didn't want to hear about any big legal moves or technical issues. They just needed a little of that human touch, so to speak, the recognition that somebody cared enough about them to return their call.

That struck something inside of me. As I had come from the client pool rather than law school, I completely understood what they were trying to say. Again, I had come to a point where there were signposts up all along this highway, and now I was starting to take notice of each and every one of them.

*   *   *

While I got along great with the clients, I had less success with the other girls in the office. This was nothing new for me; it had happened at every job I had ever had. Here they more or less ignored me, and I did the same to them, keeping busy with the phones.

Then one day, Ed dropped a box of papers on my desk that was about to change everything again in my life.

A woman by the name of Roberta Walker was friends with this fellow Joe Rimirez, who grew up in Modesto with Karen Vititoe, Jim's wife, Ed's partner. Okay? Those are the links. At that time, Pacific Gas and Electric was pressuring Roberta to sell her house to them. She was the last holdout. Everyone else in her area of Hinkley, California, had sold to PG&E and were long gone. Joe kept on telling Roberta that before she did anything, she ought to consult an attorney, and he recommended Jim, so Roberta did call.

But Jim never returned her phone call.

So one day Karen called Ed, who finally went out to see her. During the visit Roberta kept complaining of health problems, so Ed sent her to a doctor in Los Angeles for a blood workup. The results of those tests were filed and thrown into that big box with all the other materials, all but forgotten once the personal injury department of the law firm evaluated the case as being worth

> From the very beginning of the case, just as I had lived my entire life, I didn't judge anybody. I was, as always, willing to listen, and at this stage in my life, to learn—to put my mind into gear.

about $10,000 and recommended that it be dropped. However, Ed said because of Roberta's personal relationship to Karen and Jim, the firm would continue to carry the case, and on a *pro bono* basis, meaning for no fee. So that's how the files came to me. I was absolutely the lowest person on the Masry and Vititoe totem pole.

*   *   *

I went through the material, and I had no idea what I was doing from a legal point of view, but it quickly became clear to me what the real problems in Hinkley were. I had no legal training, no evaluation skills of any type, but what I did have was that weird combination of photographic memory and dyslexia, mixed in with a healthy dose of my dad's early lessons about perseverance, concentration, focus, and commitment. From the very beginning of the case, just as I had lived my entire life, I didn't judge anybody. I was, as always, willing to listen, and at this stage in my life, to learn—to put my mind into gear.

As I went over the material in the box, I kept myself open to anything that didn't look or seem right, whatever warning signs came along.

The first thing I noticed were the results of the blood tests, and how far out of the "normal" range the white blood cell counts were. It was immediately obvious to me that something was very wrong. The next day I asked Ed for permission to go to Hinkley, to visit Roberta. Of all the people I would meet and work with on the case, Roberta was the one who would most remind me of me. We shared the same instincts. She was coming from the same spiritual place that I was. She was not a dumb woman, even though she didn't have a big old master's degree or a fancy doctor of jurisprudence. She was born and raised in Hinkley and simply didn't want to give up her home. That's all that mattered to her. She was fiercely protective of her family and held their home in great esteem. Because her goals were so simple and her compassion so real, it awakened mine, not just for her but all the people of Hinkley. I identified with them on a very deep, visceral level. I saw them as victims and became dedicated to their cause. What really got to me was how they had all wanted to live in Hinkley to provide a better life for their families, to benefit from the land, and because of it had all gotten deathly ill. In a very real sense, I could see my own spirit reflected in their hearts and minds. I vowed to do my best to help them in any way I could.

I worked on the case every day, 24/7, for almost six years, and the first four years were the hardest I've ever worked at anything in my life. I would make the long drive back to Northridge at midnight, and by the time I'd get home, the kids would all be in bed. I hardly ever saw my baby Beth awake, and I didn't get to go to any of Matt's and Katie's school functions. I'd get up early the next morning and make the long drive back, often wondering what the hell I was doing, working like that for $1,200 a month as if my life depended on it.

Then I realized that was exactly the situation—my life *did* depend on it.

You see, it all went back to what my dad said at Tommy's funeral that day, the tag line to a lifetime of moral rectitude that Dad believed was the only proper way to live. *You have to.* That was my new credo, my justification, the replanted root of my determination. I had taken on a responsibility given to me by a law firm that believed I had the ability to handle it. I was not going to let them be proven wrong. Whatever it took, I would do it. I had no choice. *I had to,* in order to prove to them, and even more important, to myself, that we were right to trust and believe, to have faith in me.

> Then I realized that was exactly the situation— my life *did* depend on it.

It was a difficult challenge, but there was something here I wanted, something I needed. Every night I'd ask myself on the way home why I was doing all of this, why I was working so hard. I finally decided that if I could just get as far as becoming a real friend to any one of these people, to provide a strong enough shoulder to cry on, then I had done my job, and to me that was worth everything.

To do this, I was determined to climb over any obstacle that stood in my way. I had challenged myself to accomplish something that, believe me, at this stage, had nothing to do with money, or fame, movies, or movie stars. No one could possibly have known that the other side of all of this was a quarter-billion-dollar settlement, or a film to be made out of what went down in Hinkley, or that Julia Roberts would play me in the film that carried my name as its title. No, the challenge was to my mind, my heart, my soul, and my gut. I was doing the right thing, that much I was sure of, and as time went by, I grew ever more confident because of it. The key to everything lay in how much I believed in myself, how much I felt in sync. And once I could say for certain I did and felt completely attuned to that notion of confidence, my days of spiritual drifting were over. In that sense, my involvement in Hinkley was as

> *I had to, in order to prove to them, and even more important, to myself, that we were right to trust and believe, to*

> **The key to everything lay in how much I believed in myself, how much I felt in sync.**

much about me as it was about anyone or anything else. And, for all concerned, this was a very good thing.

And so I continued to devote myself to the people of Hinkley. My family-inspired spiritual policies that had been until then as shattered as badly as my car had been in that intersection, started coming back together. If the insurance company had managed to get my station wagon rebuilt enough to get that old wreck running again, then so too could I rebuild the engine of my soul.

By helping these people, I knew I was helping myself as well. It was, on one level, all about their physical rescue. It was, on another, all about my moral redemption.

CHAPTER FOUR

My Inner-Strength Workout

*E*arly on in my uphill battle helping Masry and Vititoe wage war on behalf of the good citizens of Hinkley against the powerful and moneyed forces of PG&E, I experienced several frustrating setbacks. Not having any first-hand experience working with lawyers on any case other than my car accident and the visitation fight with ex #2, I couldn't understand why even little things having to do with the law took so much time, or were so difficult to accomplish, or why everybody seemed to be suspicious of lawyers and disbelieving of the evils that big corporations were, at least to me, so obviously capable of committing.

One night, after the long ride home, I came back to my house, checked on the kids and the biker, all of whom were asleep, and made myself a stiff drink. I deserved it, I told myself, and shot it back. I then went to the kitchen table, grabbed a yellow legal pad and a number 2 pencil, and began making notes on all that I had done that day. This was a fairly new experience for me, and I found that this method of writing everything down, like talking to myself, was extremely helpful.

I began with a detailed account of my time, but midway through I ripped off the pages from the pad and threw them away. At the top of the next page, I scrawled, in big block letters: HOW I WANT PEOPLE TO BEHAVE TOWARD ME!!

> *Writing everything down, like talking to myself, was extremely helpful.*

Down the left side I made a list of everything that was bothering me, wondering if somehow they were related to why I wasn't doing better on the case. These were my old and bad thoughts, under headings like "It must be my fault," or "There is something wrong with me." I put them down in a free-associative manner. In other words, I didn't let any kind of "thinking" interfere with these notions. Whatever came into my head went on the yellow pad. On the right side is where I did spend time before I wrote, trying to figure out what the logical "answers" were, the "solutions" if you will, to each challenge. Here is what I wrote that night:

I had a terrible time in school.	Not my fault. I was an undiagnosed and I'll-never-learn dyslexic.

Everyday things may still be
more difficult to grasp, but
with effort, I *can* learn.

I have been divorced
two times.

Next time, *choose better.*
Gain more self-respect, and
choose a man more worthy
of who you think you really
are. Make the third (and
lucky) man the charm!

I have three children
I am raising by myself.

Okay, I thought my exes
were going to help more, but
I guess I'm lucky that they're
my exes! I need to know I
can and should count only
on *myself.* The bottom line
is, my kids must be taken
care of. And must feel
loved. Feeling sorry for
yourself won't put food
in their tummies. Doing
something positive to help
them will help all of us!
Work harder and don't look
back!

I am so lonely
I sometimes sit in
a corner and shake.

Stop feeling sorry for
yourself! Use that energy to
find someone to share your
life with. Someone who's
interested in who you
really are instead of what
he thinks you can do for (or
to) him. And stop *shaking*.
The man you're looking for
is not going to be attracted
to that. You don't need to be
rescued. Rescue yourself.
Real men like grownup
women, especially those
who don't tremble.

I am scared to death
and very sad.

Scared of what? Your own
shadow? Or is it the
emerging feeling of your own
inner strength? Don't be afraid
to succeed. And cheer up!
Why? Because I say so, that's
why! And because you can!

What if I suffer a
relapse of anorexia?

Feed your spirit and your
soul, and it will help you
keep your body strong.

84

Strength comes from strength. We have the greatest built-in support system ever conceived. *Use it!* Read a long and difficult book. Say a deep and meaningful prayer. Have a rich dessert. Have two.

I suffer from panic disorder.

Erin, nobody can hurt you but yourself. Don't be afraid to stand on your own two feet. Make a plan of action and follow it. Simple tasks at first, if necessary, that will prove you can succeed on your own at something. Remember, structure is the antidote to panic. So get it together, kid, face down your fear and move on! *You can do it!*

I am so poor.

So what? Rich is just like being poor except there's even more bills and more money to pay them—but your real problems won't go away until you *solve* them. And you won't solve them until you identify them. Poverty, for instance, is not a problem. Poverty is a *circumstance,* or the result of an inability to overcome the bad hand you think you've been dealt, or the run of lousy luck, or, or, or. You won't get rich by "trying" to get rich. You get out of poverty by realizing the power and abilities you already have inside of you. This is the first step to true wealth—the wealth of character!

What if I suddenly became rich?

Poor baby!

What am I searching for? Money? Power? Fame? A winning card at bingo?

No! Happiness. Money, power, and fame are not the tickets to happiness. Most often seeking them leads to disaster. Instead, seek what fulfills you emotionally. Be honest with yourself, and you will know better what you are looking for in yourself and what you are seeking from others. Bingo—now you're playing a winning hand!

This little talk-to-myself, in the form of a Q&A, had an enormous uplifting effect. I call the process my "inner-strength workout," and I recommend it for anyone stuck at an emotional crossroads, unsure of what to do, or feeling as if their arrows keep missing their targets. By the time I went to bed that night, I was ready to crash out, to get some much needed sleep, and I was eager to get back into the struggle in the morning. There was still so very much for me to do, and I wanted to get back to the case!

Which is exactly what I did.

* * *

In the beginning, I was kind of a lone soldier in the fight against PG&E, which was part of the reason I felt so insecure about what I was trying to do. I'll never forget the day the light bulb finally came on for Ed Masry. We were up in Hinkley together, sitting in a gas station, when he turned to me suddenly and said, "Who in the hell is PG&E? The local water purveyor?"

"Well, Jesus, Ed," I said, "I'm from Kansas, and even I know who they are."

"Oh? Well then, how much are they worth?"

He had me on that one. I didn't have a clue. And it made all the sense in the world to know, didn't it? When we arrived back at the home office, he called a stockbroker friend of his and confirmed the company's value to be somewhere around $28 *billion*.

As I say, the lightbulb above his head clicked to the on position.

*   *   *

Progress continued slowly. Remember, I'm the one who flunked math in school and still can't balance my checkbook. But after a careful look at some of the more basic facts and figures, even I could see that the PG&E's consultants' report was claiming that 90 percent of the chromates had been removed by agricultural use from the Hinkley water supply. They took that to mean that there would be no further health problems—an assertion I found quite amazing. I put my hand to my forehead. Common sense told me something wasn't right. Where did that 90 percent go? I had proof that the 1993-monitored well readings soared above the hazardous waste level. The obvious questions to me were, What must the levels have been 5 years earlier? 10 years? 15 years?

My involvement in Hinkley now turned to obsession. I found more documents, tracked down more people, and pushed Ed to bring in the best geologists available to back up what I suspected was true from the statistics I had put together. I have to say Ed and

I made a great team. He was coming from a legal position, and I from a moral one. He is one of those rare attorneys who will stand on principle to the end. He had, after all, mortgaged his home to help finance these investigations, even after the other lawyers in the firm said they were convinced we didn't have a case, simply because the statute of limitations had run out.

At one point Ed took me into the conference room, sat me down, and reviewed the facts of the case with me. Then he said he was feeling defeated. There didn't seem to be any end in sight, he said. His wife was fed up with all the extra time the case was taking away from his family, and on top of everything else he was jeopardizing the future of the firm. He had already sunk more than $2 million into it, mortgaging his house to continue the fight. Finally he turned to me and asked, "Well, kid, what do you think?"

I sat there for a minute, overwhelmed by the trust and faith Ed was putting in me. I looked around the room at all these books. "What are these, Ed?"

"Case law books," he said to me.

I then turned and stared directly at him for the longest time before I smiled and calmly replied, "Hey, Ed, I'm no lawyer, but if I were, and I had this kind of opportunity, looking at all these case laws that you go by, that somebody else set, I'd have to do some long and hard thinking. All the people who worked on them went out on a limb, with courage and strength, in the face of adversity, and they wound up making a difference in somebody else's life.

"Now I don't know what's going on with the business side of this thing. I won't pretend I understand the numbers. I'm not and I have never claimed to be an expert on chromium 6. And I am not an expert on law. But I do have great respect for my fellow man. And I do know these are real flesh-and-blood people, human beings in Hinkley, just like you and me, and they are suffering."

I leaned in. "Ed, what's the worst that could happen if we lose?" Of course, I was talking about the firm, not his personal investment, which was everything. He looked at me, and I could see the wheels turning. "Even if we lose now, Ed, we've already won because we've generated awareness, and in that sense you've helped them. And isn't that why you do what you do, Ed?"

He slowly began to shake his head up and down and broke into a smile. "You know something kid, you're right. Let's go for it."

That was the moment I knew we were going to see this thing through, together, all the way to the end. Whatever that end might be.

Not long after, Ed partnered up with two major law firms, Engstrom, Lipscomb & Lack and Girardi & Keese, who together agreed to invest what amounted to another $10 million worth of time and effort into the fight for Hinkley.

And in the end, we won. We were able to turn it into a case for fraud, which successfully eliminated the statute of limitations. Once that happened, we knew we were home. After four years, everyone connected to our side was both overjoyed and relieved the case was finally going to see daylight at the end of the tunnel. After a full year of the first round of 36 trials (you do them in groups), PG&E was hit with a $131 million verdict. At that point, they finally caved in, and they offered to settle all 634 cases for a single payment of a record-shattering $333 million.

*　　*　　*

The personal gratification I received from that settlement remains incalculable. No dollar figure can adequately define the level of my new-found self-esteem. I was a far different person at the end of the case than I was at the beginning. I had done a lot of growing, much of it by pushing up against an invisible wall of resistance, some of it put there by PG&E, and some of it there by my own history of unfocused, undelivered potential. Now I was on the other side, ready and able to handle any situation.

> I had done a lot of growing, much of it by pushing up against an invisible wall of resistance, some of it put there by PG&E, and some of it there by my own history of unfocused, undelivered potential.

The initial test of my new determination and resolve came from the most unexpected place and person. Ed Masry was the first to have to deal with the new me. Here's what happened.

*　　*　　*

The actual payout took almost another full year, during which Ed asked me how much of a bonus I thought I should get. I didn't

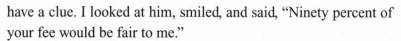

have a clue. I looked at him, smiled, and said, "Ninety percent of your fee would be fair to me."

He laughed. Thank goodness.

The day he came into my office and handed me a check for $2.5 million, I was, for one of the few times in my life, absolutely speechless. And then I started crying, bawling uncontrollably like a baby.

"Kid," he said, "what's going on?"

I reached over my desk, hugged him, and said, "I don't think you realize what you've done for me."

"Oh yeah? What about what you've done? You're a very special lady, Erin. You're a hero."

I will never forget that moment. *Ever.* It was the culmination of so many things in my life. Finally, after years of frustrating failure, of rejection and indifference, of being judged for what I looked like rather than who I was, I felt empowered. Because I had managed to empower *myself.* I had finally discovered the source of what had always been there—my inner strength, my spiritual and moral foundation, my unshakable belief in the power of right over the evil of wrong. I had done an extraordinary thing with no other tools than my own conviction. Once I had found the proper focus for my abilities, in this instance the Hinkley case, everything else slowly fell into place.

> I had done an extraordinary thing with no other tools than my own conviction.

In truth, although it's the first thing everybody always talks about, the money meant less to me than anything else about Hinkley. Of course, it was great to have, and it enabled me to do things I had never dreamed of being able to do before, but it had never been my goal, and therefore it didn't represent any sort of victory to me. I had been searching for acceptance, for validation, for *approval,* from the one person from whom it had been the hardest to get it—myself. Now, having lived this great adventure, I was ready at last for the task of turning my life into the one I always wanted it to be.

I was, finally, in control.

> I had been searching for acceptance, for validation, for *approval,* from the one person from whom it had been the hardest to get it— myself.

CHAPTER FIVE

Stick-to-itiveness

Throughout the years I worked on Hinkley, I continually called my mom and dad for help—for everything from moral support to a solid technical understanding of what it was I was discovering. Some of his input was practical; he could build one of those PG&E water plants from the ground up. However, his most important contribution to me was the steadfast presence of his moral strength. Whenever things got particularly tough for me and I'd say something like, "Oh, Dad, I just can't do this," he would remind me that I *had* to, and therefore should "press on."

Then, on one of their many visits to the house, I learned something else from my mom, the journalist. She called it "stick-to-itiveness." Don't worry, it's a real word. Webster's dictionary defines it as "a noun, meaning a propensity to follow through in a determined manner; dogged persistence born of obligation and

> "Stick-to-itiveness: a noun, meaning a propensity to follow through in a determined manner; dogged persistence born of obligation and stubbornness."

stubbornness." Don't you just love this word? I certainly do, not just for the way it sounds but for what it means.

I can't tell you how many times I thought about packing it in with my life as well as Hinkley, giving up on both, admitting defeat, and running away. There were days, months, years even when everything felt so overwhelming I didn't know which way to turn.

For the longest time, like most people, I confused *effort* with *stick-to-itiveness*. As my mom pointed out to me, there is, in fact, a huge difference between the two. Effort points you in the right direction, she said. Stick-to-itiveness is what keeps you there.

Here's an example of what she meant. Think of a man lost in the desert near a pond, with only one sack to carry water with him on his journey to rescue and salvation. His problem is to figure out how to transport enough water to get him out of the sands and back to civilization. So he fills the pouch with water and walks as far as he can without drinking any, then digs a hole and empties three-fourths of the pouch into it. He uses the last quarter to get him back to his starting point.

The next time he goes out, he does the same thing, only when he reaches the water hole, he uses half of that water to get him farther out, fills up the hole with some of the pouch water, and saves the rest to get him to the next hole. He does this repeatedly, until he has made a series of leap-frog rest stops, constantly digging and filling new holes, until finally, lo and behold, he has walked himself straight out of the desert. It was effort that got him to the first hole, but it was *stick-to-itiveness* that brought him home. The point I'm trying to make is that you have to hang in there and keep going no matter what obstacles you run into and no matter how insurmountable they seem.

To develop stick-to-itiveness, you have to get around your biggest stumbling block, which is ego. It's always a danger when our egos kick in, but if you can recognize that for what it is, you can make it work in your favor when the other side trips over theirs first. This is exactly what happened with PG&E. They believed nobody was big enough to bring them down, certainly not Ed Masry or some kooky big-busted blonde without a law degree in cha-cha heels and a leather skirt. As I remember the story, big Goliath believed the same thing about little David. The point is, don't be intimidated by the other guy, or the next one, or the one behind him. Don't confuse false ego with real empowerment. If you believe you're right, as we did when Ed, the people of Hinkley, and I took on PG&E, stand up and fight for your place in the sun. If you believe you can do it, hang in for the whole 15 rounds because even if you don't win, you will have earned the respect of everyone in the fight, including yourself, and in

> If you believe you're right, stand up and fight for your place in the sun. If you believe you can do it, hang in there for the whole 15 rounds because even if you don't win, you will have earned the respect of everyone in the fight, including yourself, and in that sense you will have prevailed.

that sense you will have prevailed. You will have demonstrated stick-to-itiveness, and for that reason alone you will have won.

*   *   *

In my own life, I learned how to focus my determination by coming to understand what boundaries I could and couldn't cross with my dad. He had a very clear sense of what was right and what was wrong, and of the notion of limits. Stick-to-itiveness requires focus, a narrowing of goals, in order to be successful. He developed this sense of focus growing up with his parents, and I have tried to pass it along to my own children. I am forever pointing out to them how, in their struggles to achieve, there are certain lines that they mustn't go beyond, because if they do, it will dissipate their strength, their focus, their determination, and eventually their will to succeed.

Going along with that, I have learned that I don't have the answers for everything and that this is not a sign of weakness or failure. I also know I can't look for answers from others, from those around me, because I'm the only one who walks in my shoes. I wish I had taken the lessons that my dad had taught me and made them a part of my way of living so many years earlier than I did, but at least I didn't go through my entire life oblivious to my inner self. One of the most important lessons to learn is that each one of us, in our own way, impacts everyone else, whether we are aware of it or not.

For instance, we all search for happiness, each and every one of us, but see it incorrectly, in the wrong things, which is why so few of us can find our way out of our own deserts. Money, power, fame—these are not the essential goals for happiness. If anything, focusing on those will keep you even further from the realization of your dreams. Money may buy you some temporary degree of satisfaction, but it certainly doesn't bring happiness. Think of all those who won big settlements in the Hinkley case but who suffered and continue to suffer from the effects of all that chromium 6 in their water. Seeking fame often means giving up the necessary honesty to be true to yourself because you want to provide the idealization of other people's images. As for power, that is simply lusting after control, most often out of a fear you really don't have any—power or control.

The only way to find happiness is to be true to yourself and to let all the rest of it—the money, the power, and the fame, should it one day come your way—be part of the result of your own, individual, inner search for true identity and self-worth.

> I see my future as bright, even with everything that has happened to me, both good and bad, because I have proven all the "experts" wrong.

Forget what others may say or think about you. I see my future as bright, even with everything that has happened to me, both good and bad, because I have proven all the "experts" wrong. When I was a child suffering from undiagnosed dyslexia, everyone told me I'd be lucky if I graduated from twelfth grade. I recently came across a copy of the *Lawrence Journal-World,* my hometown newspaper, where one of the reporters interviewed several of my teachers and childhood friends and quoted them as saying that they never would have expected this kind of success from me. I thought to myself, you see, Erin, this goes right to the heart of what you believe.

The simple truth is, every person is *unique,* and success doesn't always mean uniformity, *or conformity.* Everyone's learning curve is different. The common factor among those who succeed is *consistency,* or the ability to utilize stick-to-itiveness. What is equally as common is the fear factor among those who fail, who are afraid to see themselves for who and what they really are and accept it. For some who might be a little different, as I was, or a little rebellious, as I also was, it's even more difficult to go against the mainstream tide. Most won't or can't, and they therefore fail to develop their individuality, their talent, to celebrate what is unique about them. I call this the "the fear of individualism" that is so pervasive in our society.

I was feeling a little sick the other day and stayed home, and while relaxing, I turned on a talk radio program. I can't believe what people are saying these days, how threatened they are by anybody who acts differently from others. "Why did he do this?" or "Why did she do that?" And no one is offering any solutions, which is not surprising to me. If we seek advice on why we *shouldn't* express ourselves as individuals, what can anybody possibly say to bring us out? This need to conform is killing our most creative minds. The solution? *Stop complaining or feeling sorry for yourself about what you don't have, and instead, ask yourself what you truly want!*

Rebellion is not a bad word. It's a *misunderstood* word, especially when it comes to young people. James Dean was a rebel. Amelia Earhardt was a rebel. And so, by the way, was Thomas Edison. Ed Masry and my dad are two of the strongest rebels I've ever met. As far as I'm concerned, "rebel" is probably one of the nicer things I've been called in the last 10 years!

> *Stop complaining or feeling sorry for yourself about what you don't have, and instead, ask yourself what you truly want!*

If a child grows up in a family where everyone else is in the Navy but he or she really doesn't want to do that, the child should not be afraid to say so. I'm not calling for mayhem; we have to have rules and structure and *some* conformity, but at the same time we have to be allowed to say "I *don't* want to be in the Navy." The reason he or she doesn't, or we don't, is because of the fear factor, the repercussions for making that choice. Ultimately, of course, in the end, there aren't any repercussions because if you make a decision and *stick to it,* you will gain the respect of most people, *just for sticking to it.* It's what happened to me with Hinkley. The more I stuck with the case, the more people began to realize that, hey, maybe this lady is on to something.

One day my daughter Katie and I were having a discussion about how our lives had changed, and not necessarily for the better. "Mom," she said, "you're so quick to talk about your private life, so eager to expose things in your life . . . and to talk about how dysfunctional you've been."

Katie, remember, had gone through a lot. Plus, she had watched my life turn into some kind of media circus, with the movie, the lecture series I now give, and all the attention around Oscar time. I mean, really, it was a madhouse for all of us. During our talk, Katie finally threw up her hands and said, *"Why can't we just be a normal family?"*

A normal family. I thought about it before I said anything. Finally, I asked her to give me a definition of *normal.* It's been one year and she still can't. *And that's the whole point.* We all have these ideals in our head, our own versions of fairy tales. They work fine until good old reality intrudes, and then it's up to us to see how difficult it is to live up to our dreams, especially when it's not the same dream as everyone else's. Standing on principle is a brave thing to do, especially when your principles aren't the most popular.

I have finally come to learn that it doesn't matter to me how people see me. I've thankfully gotten beyond that. What I've been through, what I've been taught, and my hands-on experience with all those people in Hinkley who suffered, only served to validate my belief in myself even more. It's okay to question the so-called status quo, as long as you do it with dignity. In fact, I believe it's what enhances one's own dignity. And it's okay to stand by one's convictions, as long as you do it with integrity and a healthy sense of self-preservation.

My involvement with the Hinkley case did that. Everyone said I wasn't qualified to work on such an enormous undertaking, that I didn't have a four-year college education, and without that sheepskin I wasn't "equipped" to handle the load. In that sense I was "a rebel." I fell out of the pack, came around the far turn, and somehow took the lead. Maybe just *because* I didn't have the so-called necessary credentials. My determination factor outweighed my formal preparation. My emotions overrode my "smarts." My reality was stronger than my false sense of insecurity. That's what stick-to-itiveness will do for you!

*   *   *

Let's take a look for a moment at destiny and fate (some may call it *karma,* some may call it *Zen,* to me its basically all the same) in the life of any one person, or the events of any one incident. More than two thousand years ago, Heraclitus said, "A man's character *is* his fate." (See, I learned *something* in school in between dating all those cute guys.) I've always loved this statement, this realization, this vision of a deeper truth. And when I apply it to Hinkley, it gives me a chill. If one person, one event, one happenstance had been different from what it was, it's very likely none of what happened would ever have taken place. How on earth did I hook up with Ed Masry? And why, *really?* Yes, I had a car wreck, an accident that sort of symbolized where I was in my life precisely at that time. Lost at a crossroad. My life "hit" by strangers. My one major possession, my car, wrecked almost beyond repair. And out of that came all that followed.

Why did Ed Masry put that box on my desk that day? It just so happened another secretary at the office on any other day would have gotten it, but she happened to be out on this one, and so it came to me. An *accident?* What would we all have done if Roberta Walker hadn't decided to be the lone holdout? A *mistake?* And what would have happened if Ed and I had never met?

When I was in college I used to read Zig Ziglar, a well-known motivational speaker. He blew my mind when he spoke on tape about this very subject. One time I heard him say, okay, you take the same route to work every day. The one day you decide to take a different route, you have a head-on collision. Why do these things happen? Did you make a wrong decision? And who is to make that judgment? And why bother trying to figure that out?

I completely agree with that. I firmly believe there is no use in questioning destiny, that it is, in the end, the actions we do in life, guided by our character, that brings situations together, and allows us to rise to the occasion. Character is what prepares us for our moment of action, and character is what gets us through it.

> Character is what prepares us for our moment of action, and character is what gets us through it.

You want to know who I think is a *real* hero? Christopher Reeve. His date with destiny was cruel, mysterious, and completely unjustifiable, except that because of what happened to him, the rehabilitative progress for all quadriplegics has been accelerated. He is a living example of what The Reverend Dr. Martin Luther King, Jr., meant when he said, "I may not get to the mountain with you . . ." Chris may never walk again, but he has made his injury meaningful, and he has managed to sidestep the essential *meaningless* question, "Why me?" It is him, that's the hand he was dealt, and that's what he has to play out.

As I've told myself so many times, what is, *is*. For me, I have to stand by my truth and deal with all the consequences of that way of living.

According to the Zodiac, I'm a Cancer. The crab. We're known for retreating into our shell to protect ourselves from attack, to live to see another day. Self-preservation, and aggression through the very act of survival. According to Chinese astrology, I was born in the year of the Rat. Some of my "characteristics"? Compassion, insight, tenacity, affection, caring for others, caution, appeal, verbosity, influence, meddling, charisma, power and intellectual skill, moodiness. The Cancer Rat lives by her wits. A private soul trapped in the body of a public personality.

Whether you believe the fault is in the stars or in ourselves, to me it's all the same thing. Our destiny becomes the result of how we live our lives.

And I firmly believe that's why, in our lives, things are the way they are, happen the way they do, and lead us to the next higher level of our spirit and our soul.

....

CHAPTER SIX

How You Behave Toward People Is Just As Important As How You Want Them to Behave Toward You

One of the most important lessons my father taught me was the value of never trying to get away with something or lying about something to make life easier. As he knew so well, the only person we ever really lie to is ourself.

I have to admit it was a lesson I learned the hard way and one that I'm continually reminded of to this day, as I was when I entered the whirlwind of personal media coverage that is the heart and soul of Hollywood movie promotion during Academy Awards competition. My duties included the celebrity lecture circuit, where I saw how easy it actually was for some celebrities to start to believe their own often ridiculous press clippings.

I've never been one to take what others say about me and use it as an accurate or reliable definition of myself. Quite the opposite, in fact, as anyone who knows me will immediately tell you. I was still in school when I first learned one of the most primal lessons about why lying to anyone on any level is really treating yourself with no respect. Let me quickly add that if you think there are any differences between "real" lies and "white" lies, you are kidding yourself. A lie is a lie, and once you go down that trail, it becomes easier each time to tell real lies and convince yourself they're just "white" ones. At that point you have crossed a line (and then of course you are forever trying and failing to remember what lies you told to whom).

In the end, you inevitably wind up believing your own lies. This is a cumulative effect that eventually adds up to a pretty clear moral definition of who you are. You know that old expression, you are what you eat? Well, I am firmly committed to the fact that you also are what you *say*. Lie long enough, and you will start to believe your own tall stories, and then, look out, you're in big trouble!

> Lie long enough, and you will start to believe your own tall stories, and then, look out, you're in big trouble!

Here's something that happened to me once, that taught me all about the value of honesty. I had planned a trip with a girlfriend of mine to go to Chicago for a few days. I made the mistake of deciding to skip school, and let me tell you all that happened because of it. Just before we left, I was dropped off at home to change clothes. The plan was for my girlfriends to pick me up a little later. When they failed to show up on time, I became impatient and called someone to get me. Before I left, I wrote a note to my other friends—where I was, telephone number, address, even directions for how to get there. And, incredibly, I taped it to my front door for all the world to see. As fate would have it, my mother happened to come home that day for lunch—something she almost never did—and she intercepted the note.

I was already at my friend's house, having fun. As far as I was concerned, my vacation had already begun. Then the front door-bell rang. I was sure it was my girlfriends, so I started chanting, "Party! Party!" I opened the front door, and my jaw didn't just drop, it bounced off the floor. There was my mother! I took a deep breath and asked her what she was doing here. She held up the note and said, simply, "You left me directions."

It was all downhill from there. I knew immediately I had screwed up and that some serious damage had been done. I had lied and gotten caught. Worst of all, for me, my mother told my dad, and he was all torn up about it. When he asked me what happened, I lied again. He didn't say much to me, except to tell me I was going to be punished. Not only did he cancel my trip to Chicago, he grounded me for the rest of the school semester. But that wasn't the worst of it. Knowing that I had deeply hurt him was. He had put his trust in me, and I had betrayed it. And, because it was my dad, a person who worked to create a sense of honesty within his children, he knew what I had done was far

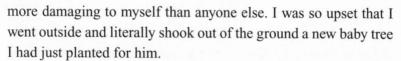

more damaging to myself than anyone else. I was so upset that I went outside and literally shook out of the ground a new baby tree I had just planted for him.

To my surprise, the next day I received the following hand-written letter. What he couldn't say the night before, he had taken the time to write down on paper. It was that important to him, and it became even more so to me. So important, in fact, I've kept it with me ever since. I carry it wherever I go, and occasionally read it to recharge my own moral battery. The letter is my dad at his best, wisest, most fatherly, and most profound. As I could never be as eloquent as my dad was that day, I thought I'd share his exact words with you now, in the hope that you may benefit from them in some measure as I have:

Dear Erin,

Riding up to Lincoln this morning, I read the enclosed in the morning Kansas City newspaper. So you see the issue is *very important* to even the President of the United States! It shouldn't be any less important to you and me.

I know last night tore you up—it did me too! But we are dealing here with a very basic principle, and you are old enough to understand it. That is, if you, your brothers and sister, your mother, and I cannot *freely and honestly* communicate with each other and believe what we are saying *and hearing,* we have lost *everything!* To do other-wise tears up the very fabric of our family, which, until you start your own, is the finest possession you will have on this earth.

Someday you and I will look back on last night and laugh and kiss about it. I know, for I used to do the same thing with my parents as I, too, used to get into trouble with them now and then. I'll have to tell you about it some day!

The thing to do now is to accept your punishment like an adult and resolve to *yourself* that it will never happen again.

There are many trips ahead of you and most of them will be more fun than the one to Chicago. So the loss is not *that* great. The loss of *our respect for each other* would have been much, much greater.

Remember, your mother and I *love* you very, very much and fervently want you to develop into an admired, honest, and respected woman.

Together, we can be *assured* it will be accomplished!

I'll see you Friday evening.

Love,
Dad

As beautiful and personal as it was, this was more than just a letter from my dad to me. *It was a turning point in my life.* I had done something I shouldn't have, my dad caught me doing it, and he took what he thought was the appropriate action. What made all the difference was that he didn't just bawl me out and punish me. He took the time to put everything into perspective, to show me where I had gone wrong. And he did it with love and affection, to make sure I knew he was with me, in my corner, even during his rather stern dressing down. It's a letter, among other things, about communication, belief in another human being, and respect. It would take me a long time to find a way to fully use his wonderful gesture to renew my own hopes, goals, and dreams, but the impact of his initial action I knew that day would be there for life.

Another thing about the letter that was so extraordinary was that it was the first time I had the realization that the quality of your life is really what you make it out to be. No matter what your past failures, you can learn and you can change. I listened to my dad, and I learned that nothing was insurmountable. After the letter, I would sit with my dad and talk to him for hours about the meaning and nature of truth. I would listen, rapt with attention to his philosophies and beliefs in the karmic power of truth, the importance of honesty as a crucial tool to better understand one's self.

Dad taught me that the way to find the truth in any situation is to look at all aspects of it, not just what makes me angry, not just what makes me sad, not just the failure of an attempt at something, but *all* aspects. Keep focused—that was a big part of the message. Always have my antennae fully extended. He wanted me to learn from everything I did, even telling him that lie, not just so I wouldn't make that same mistake again but to come to understand *why I shouldn't.*

If I could give you any single piece of advice about how to build and maintain the best part of your being throughout your own life, I

> ## TELL THE TRUTH.

would choose to simply tell you, in big, bold flashes: **TELL THE TRUTH.**

*   *   *

Long before I'd ever heard of Hinkley, because of the teachings and influence of my dad, I had a solid moral foundation. In that sense, although a lot of people thought of me as a "failure," I never did. Failure is an arbitrary assessment. Too often we confuse the concepts of "success" and "failure" with "normal" and "abnormal." Who among us is normal, anyway? According to whom? And who cares what they think anyway?

Is the janitor who lives down the street and who makes very little money a failure because he doesn't make more money than his neighbor does? Some people have a narrower comfort zone than others. So what? As long as the janitor realizes it is less important to be the best janitor in the world than it is to be the best janitor *he can be,* he's not in any way what I would call a failure. And that's the whole point. As far as I was concerned, as long as I was being, or trying my hardest to be, the best Erin I could be, I could never be a failure, no matter what anybody else thought.

The reality of life is that you deal with your circumstances as they come to you. You do the best you can, you try to stay in a positive mindset, and, as another woman I admire greatly who has also faced life alone, once said, you hang in there because "Tomorrow's another day." When things get difficult, you don't turn tail and run. If you do, you can't like yourself very much, and that to me is the only real failure.

I remember a long time ago when I was working for a company selling a shampoo line named "Lanza." It's the type of job in which a lot of rejection is a normal part of the day. One day a senior rep, who was evaluating me, watched me lose a sale. Afterward, she took my pitch apart, almost word by word, and said to me, "You know what, Erin, I'm impressed by your ability to take criticism so well."

> "I don't see it as criticism," I said. "Just another way to look at myself."

"I don't see it as criticism," I said. "Just another way to look at myself."

And that's really exactly how I felt. Rather than thinking, Okay, I just lost that sale, I must be a failure, I quit, instead, I'd stop and ask myself if maybe I did something to offend somebody. Why didn't I get that sale? I'd want to know, so I'd ask the person who turned down the shampoo line to please help me help myself by telling me why. You'd be amazed how many people will take the time to explain the reasons for doing what they do, and how often their actions have very little to do with you.

That's why, if you're out of touch with yourself, you're never going to succeed because all the negatives that you experience every day you will carry on your own shoulders, as "your fault." Instead of doing that, you need to think things through. You must ask yourself, What is it I'm trying to achieve? Why do I want to achieve it? How can I go about it?

I've never been afraid to be different, to let someone else say I'm a failure. That just doesn't matter to me. I cannot do anything I don't believe in, that goes against my code of ethics. Therefore, anything in my life I've done I've chosen to do. Oh sure, there have been times I've been frustrated, but I never let that stop me. I was frustrated not being able to finish school. Even though I couldn't learn the way other people did, I knew in my heart I had the ability to overcome my difficulties. In fact, when I tried again and stuck with it, eventually I was able to graduate from high school and go on to college, to get my associate's degree.

Likewise, I was frustrated for most of the time I was involved with Hinkley, but never felt like a failure because of it. Rather than be deterred, I would do whatever it took to keep me on course. If it meant rant and rave at somebody, then that's what I would do. Why not? The world is not going to come to an end if you let some of that anger out. Who knows, you might even be better off for it. If it meant just going home, letting my hair down, taking my clothes off, getting into a hot shower, washing my hair, making myself a drink, and listening to my favorite song, again, why not? There's nothing quite as satisfying to me as putting on a little Madonna. She's very good when you need to get yourself together. There's also a song called "Relax," by Frankie Goes To Hollywood (great name), and whenever I hear it, it gets me out of whatever funk I might be in.

Whatever I did, the next day I was ready to go out and try again. Hey, it's why they give you four downs in football.

*   *   *

A more accurate way to describe me before Hinkley was that I had my share of issues. I was dyslexic, I suffered from periodic anorexia, I was prone to panic disorders, I was seriously injured in a car accident, I had gone through two divorces, I had little child support, no decent income. And again, I never thought any of that made me a *failure*. Why would it? I knew I was a nice person, struggling to raise my three children, and even though I had no money, and no real direction in my life, I always managed to put food on their table and keep a roof over their heads. I never stole anything, hurt anybody, or deceived anyone. I always steadfastly believed that no matter what my external *circumstances* were, I was a good, moral person, and even if I didn't know exactly why, I knew there had to be reasons things happened to me the way they did.

What I didn't have until Hinkley was *focus,* a specific goal, a place to utilize my abilities and an opportunity to channel the energies of my experience. Ed Masry and his law firm, and later on the people of Hinkley, gave me that goal, focus, and opportunity.

I've never been afraid to say "I don't know," but I've also never been afraid to try to find out what it is I'm trying to understand. It's okay to not know everything. If I didn't believe that, particularly with Hinkley, I probably would have lost even more credibility with people. When I needed to, I'd simply ask someone to show me how to do something or explain a situation or a document or a memo or an ordinance to me. That was how I learned, and that was how I achieved.

I did the same thing at home. Whenever I had a problem with one of my kids, I'd ask myself why it was happening, then ask *them* if they could help me figure out what wasn't working. Then we would work together to try to fix it.

> What I didn't have until Hinkley was *focus*, a specific goal, a place to utilize my abilities and an opportunity to channel the energies of my experience.

The focus, I believe, lies in how we perceive problems. In that sense, I *love* things like clichés because they are so full of obvious truths. "The cup is either half empty or half full." You know what? That is absolutely correct! "There are no problems, only solutions." Right! "There is more than one way to skin a cat." You bet! "When the door closes, a window opens." Exactly!

"Money can't buy happiness." Now *that's* a very good one. Can I show you around my big beautiful house? Seriously, I'm not saying that money doesn't mean anything. It certainly enables you to do things you might not otherwise have been able to do, but on the other hand, you can have all the money in the world and one day be diagnosed with inoperable cancer. What's all that money going to do for you then? Let me bring this a little closer to reality. Since the 1996 settlement we got for the people of Hinkley, 50 of the original 634 plaintiffs have died, and more than a third of those deaths I believe are related to what happened because of the actions of PG&E. What good did all that money do those people? In fact, you could reasonably say it was the lust for money by the giant corporate machine that helped to hasten their end. As for me, I'd rather lose all my money than any of my dignity. I can always go out, get a job, and earn more money. It's not that easy to get your dignity back.

And here's my favorite, one I've referred to before in this book: "Do unto others as you would have others do unto you." As far as I'm concerned, it's the most important of all. You should always treat people the same way you want to be treated by them. Respecting other people will enable you to respect yourself as well. It's the primary reason that I was able to relate to the people of Hinkley and that they were able to relate to me. We shared a common hope and a common set of beliefs about what's right and what's wrong, an understanding of the essential importance of health over profit. And we knew that was all we really had. But having that awareness allowed us to keep up the good fight, to endure, and to eventually prevail. We had an advantage because we knew there had to be a solution to the problem.

I remember something a teacher once said to my class in

The Pattee family, 1960
Back row left to right: My mom, B.J. (Frank, Jr.), and Jodie
Front row: Tommy, my dad (Frank, Sr.), and me

Me with my mom, dad, and brother Tommy, and my two oldest children

My elementary school photos

In my teen years

In the 1970s

*At my wedding to
Steve Brockovich*

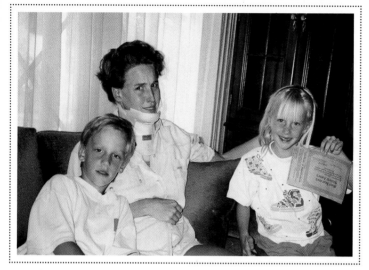

Just after my release from the hospital after the accident

Me in Hinkley

Ed Masry and me

PG&E Hinkley facility

With Roberta Walker

With my parents right after the Hinkley settlement

Happily married in Hawaii to Eric Ellis, March 1999

My kids, Shawn, Katie, and Beth

Me today! (Photo by Roman Salicki)

high school, that there is a solution to every mathematical or scientific problem, and that our job was to look for it until we found it. It was a lesson I have never forgotten. It's a great non-defeatist philosophy. And it leads to the idea that if one solution doesn't work, you simply try another. You try fifty if you have to, but you keep trying. Too many of us are content to "make an effort" at something, and then, if we haven't achieved our goal, we shrug our shoulders, lift our palms, and give up. We say that there's nothing more we can do. Well, with Hinkley, there was plenty more. And I kept trying. Every time PG&E put up an obstacle, we would try to get past it in many ways until we found the solution that worked.

That's why if Hinkley had been settled for a dollar, it would not have been a failure. It would have meant that we had prevailed, that we had proven our point. The general public would have been educated and informed, and the world would still have *known* what had happened in that town. People would go to doctors in a more timely fashion for undiagnosed illnesses, and our corporate utilities would operate under a more powerful microscope of moral responsibility. *That* was the real victory in Hinkley. *That* was what we all fought for four years to achieve. And *that* was what the town, the law firm, and I came away with. The money? That too was fine, but it was never the core issue, at least not for me or people like Roberta, who were just trying to keep themselves and their families from being murdered by willful corporate greed.

The bottom line then is that whatever life circumstances you find yourself in, your best response will always come from within. Your character will guide you through. If you have grown up to be fair, wise, and honest, when you have to take a stand in your life, you will do it with confidence and strength. And on the level where it counts, no matter what happens, you will never be a failure.

PART THREE

Who I Am Today

....

CHAPTER SEVEN

You Don't Like Salt on Your Tomatoes? Tough!

When you grow up in the Midwest, there are certain phrases that are more than just words in your vocabulary; they become a part of your vernacular. Some sound harsher than others, and none are meant to be taken literally. Rather, most are simply a colorful way of expressing a truism that is often better learned by experience first, and language reinforcement second.

One such phrase I've heard ever since I was old enough to understand language is "Tough!" (You may also know of another version, which is saved for the most special circumstances!) After the first couple of hundred times I heard my father say "Tough" to me, the phrase kind of lost all of its meaning, and it became another echoing family homily, familiar enough to hang alongside our family crest.

When I first started on the lecture circuit, I began relating a little story involving my youngest daughter, Beth, my dad, and the use of this particular phrase. Of all the topics I lecture about, this one always seems to provoke the strongest reaction. People love it, I guess because everyone can relate to either hearing it or using it, or both, at some point in their lives. It just rings true. Its meaning is clear, and it conveys exactly what is trying to be said. It's one of those expressions we all know and hear, but it still startles us by the sheer simplicity and lean toughness of its meaning.

Shortly after the film was finished, I had a million things happening to me at the same time, and they all converged on my nerve center like cars on a highway where two of the three lanes are closed down. I mean, I was an emotional traffic jam! Finally, when I couldn't stand it any longer, I clenched my fists, looked up, and shouted as loudly as I could, *"Tough!"*

Gosh, I felt better after that!

It was at that moment I flashed on the following instance, which is the one I talk about to my audiences. When Elizabeth was five years old, my mother and dad, her grandparents, had come out to California to visit for a while. I told Beth about their impending arrival and asked her if she was excited.

"No," she said. Then she put this big boo-boo lip on her face and pulled her head in.

"What? Why not? What's the matter, sweetie?"

"I don't like Grandpa anymore!"

I couldn't believe what I was hearing. Uh-oh, I said to myself. Something must have happened. "You don't like Grandpa, honey? You know Grandpa loves you."

She didn't say anything, and I let it drop, until a few days later when I was finally able to discover what was at the bottom of this. It all had to do, of all things, with Beth's love of tomatoes! One evening during one of my dad's earlier visits, he was babysitting for me, and just before Beth went up to her bedroom to go to sleep, she asked Dad if he would cut her up some tomatoes for a little snack. He said sure, and he sliced up a couple for her. As he was about to serve it, he sprinkled salt all over them just the way he always does for himself. She took her first bite and gagged! "Ugh," she cried. "THESE TOMATOES ARE AWFUL! THEY HAVE *SALT* ON THEM! I CAN'T EAT THIS!"

That's when Dad wheeled around, looked at her, smiled, and said, softly, "Well, tough."

Beth, five years old, didn't have a clue as to what he was talking about. She looked at him as if he were insane, and then she began to cry! Just then my mother walked in. She saw little Beth in hysterics, and she had no idea what was going on. Before she could say anything, she looked at Dad, who simply said, "She won't eat her tomatoes because they have salt on them. Tough."

"*I don't like them,*" Beth wailed through her tears.

"Fine," Dad said, still smiling. "I'll eat them."

Which he did.

That night, Beth got no tomatoes and went to bed hurt and angry.

Although I didn't know it, that's why Beth decided she didn't like my dad anymore. The next day I called him to see if he had any clue as to why Beth had said what she said, and that's when I finally found out what happened. When he was finished, I said,

"You know, Dad, that wasn't right. She's only five years old. I don't think you should be talking to her like that."

Silence came back to me over the phone. The next thing I heard was my dad saying to me, "Tough."

"Damn it, Dad . . ."

I put the phone down, and now *I* was hurt and angry. But you know what? It didn't last. The more I thought about it, the more I began to see why he said that to her. And once I got it, I realized how fundamental the lesson was he was trying to teach us both. It was a lesson made of what I like to call "pure Dad philosophy," and among other things, it demonstrated to me how consistent he was in his approach to everything, beginning with tomatoes and ending with . . . well, *tomatoes!*

I think his message that night may be expressed simply in a single word: *acceptance.*

You know what this means. We all go through life at one time or another beating our heads against the wall. Sooner or later there comes a time when, for whatever reason, nothing is working, nothing is in sync. *The time when traffic comes to a standstill!* At that point, you just have to wait until it starts moving again. And no matter how much you may want your car to sprout wings, there is nothing you can do except . . . *accept.* Sometimes, that's the way it is, and there's nothing you can do about it.

*   *   *

I had a "tough" custody experience recently with one of my ex-husbands. After all these years, and all our battles, we had devolved into nothing more than a game of tug-of-war over a child. He pulls a little harder, makes a few points, gains a few inches, then I pull a little harder, I get those inches back, then he pulls, and so on. No one really wins anything, the child's feelings are lost in the absurdity of the battle, and the issue itself becomes just one more game, with neither side willing to stop it. Finally, I just woke up one day, said, okay, hey, you know what? I'm not playing this game anymore. Once I realized this was a "tough" moment, I simply let it go. I bit the bullet, and by doing so I learned the "tough" lesson all over again. You can't fight every battle. It's just not worth it, no matter how much you think is at stake, or how much you're going to win. Sometimes, the real and only victory is knowing when to walk away. Or to put it another way, to eat your tomatoes with the salt on them.

> Sometimes, the real and only victory is knowing when to walk away.

Stop and think about it. "Tough" is a part of life that happens to all of us. Even lawyers who try to run extortion scams. At times there is nothing you can do about something, and you have to know when to accept your fate. You can sit in that traffic jam for hours, fuming and angry and trying to figure out why you're revving your engine and going nowhere, or you can just face the fact that that's the way it is. The only consolation is that sooner or later you will get to where you are going.

And hey, you might want to do something useful while you're waiting, like talk to yourself. Sometimes this helps even more than listening to Howard Stern on the car radio!

*   *   *

It's the same thing I'm going through with my house. Another example of respect, truth, and justice. I may win in my battle with the contractors. I may lose, but putting up the good fight and trying to get justice, in this instance for my own family, is what that battle is all about.

I guess the difference between the people who built the house and me is that I *believe* in my cause. It's the critical tilt in all these life battles. Belief is a form of confidence, which is a form of respect, which is a form of truth.

Simple as that.

*   *   *

If you want to realize any type of victory in your life, I would say the single most important rule to remember is don't be afraid to go it alone. As I see it, women are a little more openly compassionate than men. We're more physical, we want to touch and love and seek to make connections. We want to make a bond, whereas for men, at least in the beginning, it's mostly about sex. I'm not saying either

> Don't be afraid to go it alone.

way is right or wrong, or better than the other. We're just different animals in that way.

However, to make those connections, we often sacrifice what we really want for ourselves, out of fear of losing the ones we love. I see this with abused women all the time. So many of them have come to me to ask what they can do, short of leaving the man who is abusing them. They are so afraid they can't get along without him. I try to make them understand that once they make the break, they shouldn't be afraid to go it alone. I think as women we still suppress ourselves in what is for the most part a male-run world. We have made headway, no question, but hello, we're not all the way there yet. None of us is. So many of us are still intimidated, still afraid to stand up for what's right, for what we believe in, mainly because of the paralyzing fear of the consequence of having to then go it alone.

It's out of that fear that I made so many of the wrong decisions in my life. To this day I can still hear one person or another "warning" me on the day of my divorce that I was now going to be forever alone because of my decision to leave. "You're divorced twice now, you've got kids, who'd want you?"

Don't misunderstand, relationships are beautiful things, unless they stop you from being, or becoming, who you are. If that's the case, you have to face facts and move on. This is the stigma that we women carry, and it affects everything we do—the way we dress, the way we carry ourselves, the way we try to lead our lives. I read a very interesting piece on the Internet recently that totally bashed the *Erin Brockovich* movie, and not because of anything that went down in the case against PG&E but because of the way I was dressed and my language. I thought to myself, hey, I don't like this. Humanity isn't about labeling and judging. It's about charity and what's going on *inside of me*. I'm a good person, as nonhypocritical as they come, and I'm not about to be forced into being something or someone I'm not just to please one authority or another.

What if the hero of the film had been a young, bearded man in jeans and a tee-shirt, would the reaction have been the same? It makes you wonder, doesn't it? I hope it makes you think, as well.

Look at the women we revere today, all the young girls, the movie stars, the models in our magazines. These are the role-model women men are taught to go after. As the mother of one teenage daughter and another about to become a teen, I find this a bit confusing, and quite troubling, because when women in society try to emulate that very look, they're immediately labeled. By men! What is the message we're being presented? That men like the sleek, sexy, seductive women the media uses to sell products, yet when a woman decides she wants to be sleek, sexy, and seductive in the real world, boom, she's marked as some sort of slut. It's a widespread form of intimidation, a fear factor that makes us try to avoid who it is we really are and really want to be. The intimidating price for trying to be who we want to be is the fear of being alone.

And that's the crux of the problem, isn't it? We, as women, are kind of forced to bend, literally and in other ways. We bend to appease the children. We bend to appease our employers. We bend to appease our husbands. *Let's stop bending so much!*

The only defense I can see for all this compromising, this bending, is my variation of Dad's beautiful "tough" acceptance theory of one of the have-to realities of life—so let me say it again: *Don't ever be afraid to go it alone.*

....

CHAPTER EIGHT

Sublime Rhythms

I was divorced again in May 1990, an event that kicked off a particularly tumultuous year that ended tragically for me. Before it was over, the very limits of my moral and spiritual beliefs would be tested. The tumbling over one another of these events began simply enough, when, not long after I made that horrible drive through the snowstorm from Reno to Kansas, I found out I was pregnant yet again. Beth, my youngest, was born in April 1991, and that June I returned with my girlfriend to California where I first met "The Biker" at that Calabasas cantina. In September, still the same year, I had my neck surgery, and finally, at Christmastime Steve sought visitation rights, which worried me because I was single and unemployed.

As if this wasn't bad enough, it was about this time my first ex decided to reenter my life, the last thing I needed or expected. He was having a difficult time finding a place to live, and I decided to try to help him out because, after all, he was Matt and Katie's dad. I decided he could live in the garage of my cockroach-infested little house. It was pretty well set up, almost nicer than the house itself. It had been converted by the owners into a little apartment, complete with all the basic necessities, including a TV, a sofa, and a phone.

About a week after Shawn moved in, he got a job. And soon after that, he started partying after work. And if that wasn't bad enough, he also started getting obnoxious. He crossed a line when, one night, he brought some friends back to the house.

It was a horrible situation. I woke up to loud music coming through the walls of the garage. I thought the neighbors must be having a party. I heard a lot of commotion, and I went to check it out, only to find that it was Shawn and his friends. So there I was, in the midst of still more chaos. I was living with a man I wasn't in love with only because he liked the kids and wanted to take care of them. And living it up in the garage was my ex-husband. All this was going on while my second ex-husband was pursuing visitation rights.

The next day, when the dust had finally settled and I found myself still in one piece, I made up my mind that Shawn had to go. When I told him, he became miffed, and when I broke the news to the kids, much to my surprise, so were they! Now, again, I was being blamed for all the things everyone else had done. The children wanted their daddy to be with them. When they couldn't have that, and because they were too young to understand why, all the blame came down on me.

I didn't know what to do about it. Months went by while I tried to figure something out that would make everyone happy. One night, about 3:30 in the morning, I was sitting up alone in the living room when the phone rang. I never like to get a call at that hour because it's almost always bad news. The first thing I thought was that something must have happened to my dad. My heart was pounding as I picked up the phone, and I heard a man's voice identifying himself as a doctor, calling to inform me that Shawn had had a serious auto accident and had broken his neck. That meant he was a hair away from being permanently paralyzed from the neck down. He was lucky to be alive. And then, my brother Tommy, who was young, healthy, and in the prime of his life, suddenly and unexpectedly died.

I remind you of the chronology of these events to point out the sublime rhythms that are contained in the ongoing waves from the ocean that is our lives. These rising and falling waves may drown you, or wash you to shore, depending upon how you ride them. At this time in my life, the tidal waves were crashing all around, but because of the buoyancy of my spiritual uplift, I was able to somehow stay afloat, keeping my head barely but surely above water, until Ed Masry threw the lifeline called Hinkley my way and, by doing so, hauled me into the safer waters that was the case.

* * *

The idea to make a film out of my work in Hinkley began as the smallest of ripples when, in 1995, my chiropractor, of all people, a woman by the name of Pamela Dumond, found herself amused at the unlikely events that were taking place. I had first met Pamela through my sister, Jodie, when they had both lived in Chicago. After my car wreck, when I had so many ongoing shoulder and neck problems, Jodie urged me to see Pam, who had since relocated to L.A. I kept putting it off until one day I couldn't take the pain anymore and decided to give her a call.

She and I quickly became friends, and every time I went for a session, to pass the time I'd tell her stories about what was going on in Hinkley, be it my collecting dead frogs from the water ponds, the sinister activities on the part of PG&E, or my trials and tribulations with the biker and the kids. She always seemed fascinated by the whole thing, and often asked me how I was able to keep up with and handle all these different events and people. No wonder I had all this discomfort, she said. How right she was. My whole world, it seemed, was filled with nothing but pains in the neck of one sort or another.

I didn't know it at the time, but Pam was also treating Carla Schamberg, who is married to Michael Schamberg, Danny DeVito's partner in a movie production company called Jersey Films. Every time Pam saw Carla, she would fill her in on the latest episode of my life. After months of collecting these stories, Carla finally said, "I simply have to meet this woman!"

A few days later Pam told me she had this friend in the movie business and could she tell her some of my stories, not letting on that she already had. "Sure," I said. "Why not?" And not long after that, Carla sent word through Pam that she would like to meet me.

I said fine. I had Carla set it up, and I promptly forgot all about it until the day it took place. That became a day I will never forget.

I went to Carla's house and rang the front door bell. When she opened it, I could see her double-take stare. It was a familiar look, one I'd seen most of my adult life. For there I was, this big-haired Amazon in four-inch stiletto pumps, leather miniskirt, and leather bustier. To make matters even more startling, Carla is a smallish woman, and I was literally towering over her. The look on her face reminded me of the one Roberta had on hers the first time I called on her in Hinkley.

We stared at each other for a few very long seconds, and then we both broke out laughing, which immediately vented the moment of all its tension. For the rest of that first day together, we had a blast. I mean we really hit it off. We spent five hours together talking, hanging out, getting to know each other. It happened to be my birthday, and because of it, the tone of the meeting took on something of a celebration. At some point during our talk, Carla said she would simply love to make a movie about my involvement with Hinkley, complete with all the various intrigues and characters she had been hearing so much about from Pam.

The next day Carla told her husband he had to meet me, that I had an incredible story that was a natural for the movies, and also a perfect vehicle for Julia Roberts.

"Yeah, sure," Michael said, as in "never going to happen." Because he was a successful producer in the film business, he heard this kind of thing about a thousand times a day. Everyone from the parking lot valet to the head of production had a "perfect Julia Roberts" movie waiting to be made, if only so-and-so could read the script. Now he was hearing it from his wife, who was just about the last person he wanted or needed to bring movie ideas to him. He brushed the whole thing off in favor of his real life, and he quickly forgot about what he thought was a fantasy of Carla's.

However, she didn't forget about it at all. Quite the opposite. Every day she kept at Michael in much the same manner that I had with Jim Vititoe and Ed Masry when I'd wanted a job answering their phones. And eventually, just as Jim and Ed had with me, for no other reason than to get her off his back, he said he would bring the idea to his partners and agreed to more or less "give" her the project if she could get it going to the point where it made sense to Jersey Films to get behind it. It wasn't much, but it was a start.

And it was all that Carla needed. I do remember thinking what a perfect match we were, if for no other reason than that I didn't have a clue as to what we were doing or what I was about to get into in trying to make a movie. She became the executive producer, and soon I was being called in to meet with Danny DeVito, Michael's partner and one of the principals of Jersey Films.

That day, however, did not begin well for me. I woke up with a bad head cold and a touch of laryngitis. Because of it, at the meeting, for a change, I let someone else do most of the talking. Danny, who loves to tell stories, was like the Energizer Bunny that day. He kept on going and going, stopping only occasionally to wait for me to say something. *Anything.* When nothing came out of my mouth, he'd start again. Finally, after more than an hour had passed, in a calm and orderly fashion, he asked me if I ever spoke. I responded in this tiny, raspy voice, something like, "Sure I do."

He looked at me, again for a long time, and then asked, in a slow and steady voice, "You don't really talk like that, do you?" I shook my head, we both started laughing, and we both knew it was going to be okay.

*   *   *

This first meeting with Danny and Jersey Films happened in 1995, while the Hinkley case was still in progress. It would take, in fact, another five years before the picture actually got made, nearly as much time as it took to resolve the case itself. During that time all of us were certain there was no way it was ever actually going to make it as far as opening night. For example, just getting the rights to everyone's real-life characters had taken two forevers. Carla is a very superstitious person and doesn't like to talk about anything until it happens, which is why from the beginning, she made it very clear to me that just because she was *thinking* about buying the rights to my story, that didn't mean they were automatically going to be picked up, or that there was any guarantee the film was ever going to actually get made. More often than not, she explained, these types of projects—which she described to me as "slightly off-the-wall," and "not easily pegged" the way typical Hollywood love stories and action-adventures are—wind up getting shelved, and that's the end of it forever. Of course, she said, our film, while not at all typical—we were more of an odd type like *Silkwood* or *China Syndrome*—had elements of both a love story and an action-adventure, which might hold the key to getting it green-lighted (given the financing to shoot) by a major studio.

A couple of months after my first conversation with Carla, I received a call from Jersey Films that really swept me away. The company was advising me to get a lawyer because our project had been green-lighted—they were going to go ahead with the movie. I was to receive $30,000 up front for the rights to my story, and at that point I thought, hell, even if the film never gets made, I'm thirty grand ahead of the game!

So, okay I thought, bring on the cameras!

My joy was short-lived. Early on, even before the writer, Susannah Grant (who would eventually be nominated for an Academy Award for her screenplay) was on board, someone had come up with the brilliant idea of a romantic connection between Ed Masry and me, as a way to make the film more "conventional." This just about blew me away. Of course, I rejected this notion out of hand, and I let everyone know in no uncertain terms that to me this was the deal-breaker. Why? Quite simply, besides the fact that there wasn't a single *shred* of truth in it, that kind of Hollywood garbage trivialized all that I had worked so hard to accomplish in Hinkley. Ironically, of course, this was exactly the same plot a couple of my exes hatched a few years later during their attempted extortion.

Both instances taught me something quite basic about human nature. If you stop and think about it, how far apart, really, was this concept of what the public would believe, would *need* to make "Erin's" story acceptable, and what my exes thought. It was the story of my life, as seen by everyone else except me, the person who lived it, crudely and distortedly played back right in my face all over again. I didn't have the ability to do what I had actually done. I didn't have the smarts. I didn't have the legal education. I didn't have the guts. Besides, I looked "easy." For all those "reasons," to both Hollywood and my two ex-whatevers, my true accomplishments had to be based on something other than who I was. Lady Luck or the skill to be able to sleep my way to the top. So you see, in the end, after all that I had been through with Hinkley, to many of those who already knew the story, including some very talented film people, no one really had any true understanding or actual respect for what I had managed to accomplish. At both times when this scenario popped up in my life, during the making of the movie and the extortion trial, the fact that anyone would want to bet on that version of the story both amazed and depressed me. What's more, I'm sure there are a lot of people to this day who still won't, or can't, believe the truth of what happened, or my part in it, because they can't see my hard work, my good ethics, and my spiritual policies because they're too busy staring at my big chest.

Of course, I made it clear that if anything like that was even remotely suggested in the script, I would get out of this contract so fast, the wind from the slamming of the door behind me might knock over everyone left in the room.

The director Steven Soderbergh was against that sort of thinking from the beginning, to his credit, and he supported my decision not to want any trash like that in the movie. From that point on, whenever anything even remotely like that came up, he'd come to me with the studio's "version" of events and try to find out the essential truth behind what had actually happened. I'll give you an example. Remember the scene when Julia is in the bar, and it seems as if some guy from PG&E is trying to pick her up? It was a very tricky moment to capture, and it could have gone in a lot of not-so-great places.

In truth, at this stage of the case, things had not been going very well. In the original script, my character is sitting in a bar, just as I had done, but the scene was written to make it look like that fellow was hitting on me, just trying to pick me up and get laid. Steven came over to my house one day to talk over that scene. Something was bothering him about it, and he wasn't quite sure what it was. His instinct for the truth was as strong as ever. That's when I said, "That's because it never happened, at least the way it's written in the script."

I then told him what had actually taken place. "Yes, I was in that bar," I said, "the Sit 'n' Bull Café. It was about a hundred degrees out, and I was having a beer wondering just what the hell I was doing in this godforsaken place. I never saw my kids anymore, I was sure I was never going to be able to prove that PG&E knew what they had done to the people of Hinkley, I was tired, and I was spinning my wheels. As I downed my brew, a dozen horseflies buzzed around my head. You know what, Erin, I said to myself, your life really sucks!

"And *that's* when this PG&E employee by the name of Chuck Ebersohl came over to me. Chuck had seen me at employee meetings, I had already signed up his daughters to be part of the case, and he knew I was good friends with Lillian Melendez and some of the other PG&E employees. So he decided to take a chance. He came over to me, and maybe because I looked so forlorn, said, 'You know, Erin, I really like you.'

"Now, I'm looking at him, wondering where he's coming from, when he leaned into me, not wanting anyone else to hear what he was about to say, and kind of whispered, 'I feel like I can tell you anything.'

" 'What's on your mind Chuck,' I said.

" 'You think it would be important to you if PG&E told me to destroy some documents?'

"*Ohmigod!* I thought to myself, I've got to call Ed right now! I told Chuck I had to go to the bathroom, and I asked him to wait for me. As soon as I was out the door, I desperately tried to get Ed on the phone. When the girl at the switchboard finally put me through to him, I told him what I'd just learned, and he was so excited, he wanted me to take Chuck's declaration right then and there. Of course, I didn't know what the hell he was talking about."

At that point Steven smiled and said, "Ah, see, there's nothing better than the truth. *That's* what that episode is really all about, and that's how we're going to tell it."

What a prince. After that, I knew I wasn't going to have anything to worry about with this movie. Not long after, the absurd notion of my having some kind of Hollywood-fantasy romance with Ed Masry, or with anyone in the film for that matter, was quickly dropped and never brought up again, in favor of a better, more truthful version of the characters and events as they *actually* happened. Anything that anyone tried to fictionalize was eventually restored to a more faithful representation of what actually happened.

Something I've believed in my whole life, and that had been proven to me all over again by Steven and Jersey Films and Universal is that there really *is* nothing better than the truth!

* * *

Up until the day the film opened, working on it was like watching a tidal wave that had begun so far offshore that it looked as though it would never reach the mainland. I hardly told anyone about the movie out of fear of being committed to an institution for having finally convinced my friends and family I had gone totally insane. Instead, once Hinkley was settled I quietly moved on to a new case, Kettleman v. PG&E, another chromium 6 situation that is still ongoing. After Hinkley, PG&E, in a move I have to believe was made at least in part to stop the flood of lawsuits we had brought, declared a very well publicized bankruptcy. But guess what? They're not broke at all. Far from it. They simply funneled a lot of their funds to a parent company. As a result, we've had to wait a little while with Kettleman, while all the money connections are made. We have a thousand plaintiffs in this one, nearly twice as many as with Hinkley, and we will fight, just as hard. PG&E will always be PG&E, and they will have to be held accountable for all the damage they've done. The facts in Kettleman are as clear as they were in Hinkley, and I am 100 percent certain that within the coming two years, justice will once again be served.

* * *

As for the film, how fortunate I truly was to have worked with Jersey Films. This is a company, smack in the middle of "bad and dangerous" Hollywood, that stands for everything I believe in. They had the right kind of respect, integrity, and honor to see my story for what it was and to produce it the way it needed to be made. Just as much as Ed Masry and Jim Vititoe had changed my view of the legal system, so did Carla, Michael, Danny, and Stacey Sher (another partner at Jersey Films) change my opinion of Hollywood. They understood the at-times less-than-great situation in Corporate America, and they appreciated the value of a story about a woman—*a single mom*—taking it on, and the true worth of the people of Hinkley. They told our story with great dignity, and I believe they set an example for the kind of films Hollywood can make. They allowed audiences of real people to sit back and for once go, hey, that's me up there on that big screen, *that's my story!* I'm the single mom, or that's me, I'm divorced, or that's me, I like to dress like a babe, or that's me, I live on a toxic dump. *The film is relatable because it's real life.* Too often, we're presented with a fantasy world in the movies that in real life just doesn't exist. I love movies, real movies like *The Insider,* movies *about real life.*

Let's be our own heroes. Let's write our own endings to the one movie we all have leading roles in, the screenplay of our lives, set on the planet we share, starring all the people we should get along with and treat as we want to be treated. Why should we lie awake at night worrying about what some flavor of the day is starring in this Friday night? I for one am not into idolizing those who don't exist.

> Let's be our own heroes.

I'd rather idolize the real people of the world, the unsung heroes fighting the evils of Corporate America, those who have no choice but to live in a world that others seek to take advantage of.

It would make one hell of a movie, don't you think? Or one that was already made by Steven Soderbergh and company.

....

CHAPTER NINE

You Can Rescue Yourself!

In my wildest dreams I never thought it possible I'd be giving lectures to thousands of people who would come out just to hear what I had to say. At first I was afraid it might simply be a misery-loves-company situation, but that was only that—my fear doing the thinking for me. The truth is, it is wonderful to be able to get out there and meet so many men and women just like myself who are seeking ways to empower their own lives, to tap the rich resources they already have within their spirit and their soul. If I can use my own life as an example to help other people understand how to make that round trip—to the inside and back out again—then I feel I have done something worthwhile. It is a joy for me to try to help you begin to understand how it is possible to live the best life you are capable of. Believe me, this is a very, very good feeling.

I've also enjoyed all the perks that are part of any lecture series. I've seen a lot of cities I've never been to before, I'm paid well, and people seem to know who I am wherever I go.

I was at an airport recently, and I decided to grab a quick bite before my plane boarded. I had been running around since dawn and I was starving! Because the restaurant was packed, I had to stand next to the garbage cans, okay with me, while I tried to shovel some food into myself. As I was eating, I looked up, and there was a guy on the other side of the trash cans staring at me. Our eyes met, and in a whispered voice he said, "I know who you are."

"You do?" I said, smiling. "Who am I?"

"You're . . ." And then his voice got even tinier, as if he didn't want anyone else to know our little secret: *"You're Erin Brockovich!"*

I replied in a similar sotto voice, "Okay, and I won't tell if you won't tell!"

I've also had people look at my credit card and go, "Oh My God! It's . . . *her!*"

Or even better (or worse), "Hey, you've got the same name as that movie!"

* * *

For the first time in a very long time, I feel truly wonderful, like a whole human being. Even with everything that followed the Hinkley settlement and the movie—the extortion, the house problems, all of it—I know I'm a better person than I was before the case because I found a way to find the power of the truth within myself and use it to guide me through good times and bad with my head held high.

And because I am truly connected to my inner self, I no longer have to carry the false burdens of guilt and shame for some of the things I've done. For instance, I used to feel sad that because I had been divorced twice, I had somehow deprived Matt and Katie, and Beth too, of a real father. The better way to see that was that I tried to help them every step of the way. Now, the old Erin would have felt even worse trying to find out what she had done wrong. The new Erin knows enough to deflect the onslaught, to know it isn't her fault, and to walk away from all the guilt, believing only in the future and secure that it will be bright and positive. As it turns out, Katie has recently decided she wants to get to know her dad a little better. That's fine with me.

One of the most important aspects of my being able to get out of the past has been to meet the man who would become my third husband.

His name is Eric. To begin with, he came into my life at a time when I was having difficulty setting up my own boundaries. Being an outsider, he was able to help me establish a new reality. I'm a headstrong person, and I usually don't respond to anybody's telling me what to do, especially in love and romance. Bossing me around and protecting me are two different things.

Eric either didn't know this about me or didn't care. One of the first things he did when we became involved was to tell me that the relationship problems of the past were over. "From now on," he said, "we'll face the future together." That was a delight for me to hear. I was so tired of having to watch out for my own back-side 24 hours a day, seven days a week. I had been through the mill, and I sensed with Eric that I had finally earned the right to be free and happy. I was ready at last to take full responsibility and some credit for all that I had accomplished. I was in my late thirties and in a relationship I was determined to make work.

I knew I could be grateful for a lot of things. I was grateful for my children, for the experiences I'd had with my first two husbands. No matter how tough things had gotten, I had managed to hang on, and with dignity. I am proud that I never chose to go on welfare, even when it looked as if we might not have enough food or shelter. One way or another I was always able to stand on my own two feet, and I never confused right with wrong, or allowed such confusion to lure me into easier ways of making a buck. The only problem for me that remained, something that Eric could see much more clearly than I could, was that I *had* completely moved on, so there was no reason to continue to associate with anyone from my past on any level except when it came to the children. Unfortunately, with some people, when they smell a good thing, they keep coming back for more.

Only when the kids were a little older, and the movie came out, did I begin to realize that a lot of what had gone down had become a very old dance for me. As for Eric, it didn't take him that long to say that if I couldn't bury the past, our future would be unable to grow.

That was a wakeup call for me. It was a very easy decision. After Eric's caution, the very next time the past showed up on my front door, Eric took the reins, and it was no longer welcome in our house.

He told the same thing to the biker. Remember, he and I were never married, never really involved, and he had been paid for his time and trouble. Even Beth, whose crying had led me to allow him back in that time, had had enough and wanted it to stop. In truth, all our lives were changing. Later on, I got a call from one of my exes who said, "Erin, this movie has gone to your head. You've changed."

I found that quite an amusing comment. "I haven't changed at all," I said. "I was tough before the film, and I'm tough now. The same as I was in high school. If anyone's changed, it's you. You don't like what's happened to me, and it's made you even angrier than you always were."

Furthermore, I said, I'm in love and interested in looking in only one direction—the future.

*   *   *

Eric is the kind of person I wish I had married in the first place. We first met in 1994, and I wouldn't have minded dating him then, except that I was living with the biker at the time, working every minute of my waking life on Hinkley, and I didn't have enough time to take a pee, let alone become involved with a new man.

Time passed, the case was settled, and the movie was getting closer to becoming a reality when one day in August 1998 Eric came looking for me again, and, boy, this time was I ready for him! What had happened was, he had gotten a message to me via a mutual friend asking if I would have dinner with him. I said yes, and, well, what else can I say except that we have been together ever since.

Marriage to Eric is everything I had always hoped marriage could be. We hold hands, we laugh, we talk, we hug, we share. I'd heard about real love my whole life, and I was always the first one to laugh at it, but when that angel's arrow landed square in my heart, I instantly knew what the feeling was that makes the poets rhyme.

Although I had failed at it twice, I never wavered in my belief that the idea of marriage could work. The keys to having a happy marriage, I know now, are respect, honesty, and friendship. Take it from me: Liking one another is important. I had a boyfriend once who told me that while he loved me like crazy, he really didn't like me very much. Needless to say, that relationship ended rather quickly. I can honestly say that while I was emotionally involved to some degree with my exes, looking back I realize that had I addressed more of my own reasons—like the fear of being alone, or how I would be perceived by my peers, by my parents, or by society in general—I might not have made the choices I did. I may have been too young to know better, or too old not to, and with the biker, well, he was *there* (and I wasn't). This

> Take it from me:
> Liking one
> another is
> important.

time, it's different. I *like* Eric, and that is the crucial element that makes our relationship work.

Everything else includes the day-to-day compromises, mutual respect for each other's feelings and emotions (that's *huge*), and sharing—not just *things* but feelings and emotions—and being able to hang out and hang loose. It all comes out of that one essential, *liking* each other. My parents have been married to each other for 55 years, and they are the best living proof of what I'm telling you.

This is not to imply that Eric and I are perfectly happy with each other all the time. The true test of a relationship doesn't happen when everything is going well. Rather, when things are rocky, *that's* when you find out what your relationship is made of. When Eric and I argue, I want to stay in his face, while Eric likes to leave. I had, unfortunately, learned early on in my marriages when something was off, you stayed and fought about it, while Eric preferred to leave situations alone, to allow them to cool off. A real breakthrough came for us when I learned to back away from an ongoing confrontation, and he adjusted his behavior, to try and hang in with me so as not to feed my fears of abandonment. In that way, I learned to respect his need to be alone, and he learned to respect my need to talk things through. I can't emphasize how important this has been for our marriage, for our romance, *and for our friendship.*

This is also the first time in my life I've altered the pattern of my marriages. Both times before, I was, essentially, an emotional adult child, and I acted like it. This time, I'm an adult married to an adult, and we both try to behave like grownups to solve whatever issues may come between us.

In hindsight, I can see now that one of my earlier mistakes was not believing in myself enough to go it alone, thinking I had to have a man to support me, to comfort me, to protect me. Everything but love me. I know now that we can all go through life alone, if we have to, and that it's not such a bad thing. We can overcome all the obstacles—trials, tribulations, financial woes, learning disorders, all of it—by ourselves, *if we have to*. What's that old expression, you're born alone, you die alone. Well, I think sometimes you have to go through life alone. That's just the way it is. *Tough!*

> One of my earlier mistakes was not believing in myself enough to go it alone, thinking that I had to have a man to support me, to comfort me, to protect me.

And then, when you're ready, you can have the kind of relationship that I'm talking about. Being able to learn from my past mistakes, I am, for the first time, emotionally ready to be in an adult relationship. I now know how great it is that when I'm feeling down, there is someone who is willing to hold me, to tell me that everything is going to be all right. Being truly in love is a privilege to be had only *after* you've learned to love yourself. It is only when you become your own support system, that someone you love is free to journey along with you to a much deeper and more profound place in your spirit and your soul.

The most important value of my marriage to Eric, then, is *the bond*. The uniqueness of two individuals who have a bond that no one can break is something that has finally become a reality to me. I never had it before with any man. I

> *Being truly in love is a privilege to be had only after you've learned to love yourself.*

have it with Eric. Going along with that, I'm very specific in my needs and desires for things I require from a man. First on my list is loyalty. If I don't have that, if a man cheats on me (or if I cheat on my man), it breaks "the bond." I've never broken the sacred commitment of intimacy to any man, and I know I never will. To this day, I'm not sure enough people understand either what they have *or* what they stand to lose until it's too late and everything is gone.

I'm not afraid to learn from my mistakes, to look at the wrong decisions I've made, to examine the impact they've had on my life and others, so that I can take steps to ensure I don't do the same stupid things over and over again. I guess that's why I'm not afraid to take this look at my own life. It's the best way I know of to distill the important lessons I've learned. I find it is a wonderful thing to finally be able to admit in these pages things I've done that I regret, that went totally against every moral fiber in my body, like having that abortion. As I say, I'm not perfect, I've made mistakes, and I've paid some heavy prices, but at least I've tried to learn from my past, to let it help me make better choices so as to not to repeat the errors of my ways.

That is why, for everything that has gone down, I can honestly and happily say that I wish no one in my life any harm or ill will. Just as I have to, so must they all live with the impact and the consequences of what they have done in and with their lives. Whatever bad meat you have bitten into, you will have to deal with its journey through the system of your soul.

*   *   *

Another word for *bond* is *respect.* I had never experienced it before. Any time something good happened in my life, it was always taken by everyone around me as some kind of a fluke. I must have been born under a lucky star, I heard that a *lot,* or I must have somehow used a little sex to maneuver myself into a better position. It almost never occurred to anyone that I just might have had something positive and forceful to do with my own fate.

Eric and I benefit from a mutual respect. Although our marriage is good, in the beginning, we were both frightened of making the seven-league leap. I had been there twice before; he is four years younger than me; my career is on an arc. But there are times when you can be paralyzed by the thought process, by the weighing of every last differential, by allowing hesitation to interfere with action. Merry-go-rounds are tricky; sometimes you think you're moving when you're really standing still, sometimes you're standing still when you think you're moving, and sometimes even when you're moving you're really only going around in circles. Eric and I decided early on, even if we scraped our knees, bruised our egos, or fell flat on our faces, we were going to take deep breaths, link pinkies, and, one, two, three, jump off that carousel into our future together.

Sure, along with the day-to-day struggles, there are moments when you might stop and say, What am I doing here with him? How did I get into this mess? But Eric is the kind of man who can help me get through such moments. He doesn't get as dizzy, and his shoulders are broad enough to carry the day.

*　　*　　*

I have to tell you, though, that where we have come in our marriage has not always been that easy a journey. The first two years were a bit tumultuous, as old and bad habits are sometimes hard to break. We didn't always see eye to eye, and sometimes out of sheer frustration he would leave and go for a drive. That's when the old fears would creep back inside of me and play hide and seek with my soul . . . *I'm forty years old, I have three children, I've been divorced twice, who in the hell is going to want me* . . . That would last until the better side of me took over, and only then could I smile and think to myself, *Eric, if you can walk away from me, from our life, don't let the door hit you in the ass on the way out. If I have go it alone, you know what? I'll still survive, I'll still make it. I like and I believe in myself, flaws and all. For every ship that sets sail, another one comes in behind it.*

What's so hard for people to learn—and for me too—is that when you take that kind of position, when you deal from strength as an individual, those trying to play with your head and your heart will most likely stop and reconsider you in a whole new light. And what's the worst thing that could happen? The two of you will continue to disagree? So what? Believe me, neither of your worlds is going to come to an end. More likely, it will take you to a new place much more suited to where the both of you would rather be.

*   *   *

Eric moved into the house that September 1998, and, of course, all my friends and acquaintances were concerned. Including Ed. Although now he can't imagine a better man for me, at the time he was a little worried about the speed of this relationship. Besides, Eric was an aspiring actor and a late-night country-western music DJ, not exactly great hours for someone who wants to be involved with a high-maintenance person (moi) and help raise a family.

But there he was, I loved him, and no one was going to be able to do anything about it. And when my dad finally met Eric, he actually liked him! This was a first in my life. And the kids accepted him too. Beth, especially, bless her heart, fell absolutely head over heels for him!

Even before he moved in, Eric proved how much he was going to be there for me. One of the hardest things I'd ever had to do came about in May 1999, when I took Matt to Sorenson's Ranch

Boarding School in Koosharen, Utah, to begin a recovery program from drugs and drinking. I had tried everything I could think of, even letting him live with his dad for a while. I was afraid there was nothing I was going to be able to do to prevent him from continuing down a very bad road. Now that I had received my bonus money, I knew the first thing I wanted to do with it was to get Matt into serious rehab, and then maybe send him to boarding school. A lot of people who should have known better simply figured now that I was "rich," I was getting rid of a major headache so that Eric and I could live it up. Well, for their information, without

> *Until I removed them from their present environment, they wouldn't have a hobo's chance in hell.*

the $2.5 million, I might not have been able to save my kids' lives. I'm not a psychiatrist. I'm not a drug counselor. At some point I had to concede that both Matt's and Katie's problems were too serious for me to solve without help. I had already begged, pleaded with, and threatened them. Nothing worked. Finally, the only thing I could do was to get them into the best professional programs available. Their pediatricians had told me the same thing, that until I removed them from their present environment, they wouldn't have a hobo's chance in hell.

The night before I was scheduled to take Matt to Utah, I was a basket case. Eric stayed with me on the phone from L.A. for three hours trying to help me get a hold of myself, which I wasn't having much luck doing. The next day, when we finally arrived in Utah, the last look on that boy's face is one I'll never forget. The counselor had warned me in advance that once I'd dropped him at the gate, I shouldn't look back, but I just couldn't help it. As soon as our eyes met, the tears came streaming down both our faces.

And then he was gone.

I didn't see him again for nearly a year. When we finally reunited, he was a completely different person. He had done a lot of growing up, and the maturity was written all over his handsome face. One of the first things he told me when he came home was that he gone through some changes and felt he had grown up. It was a very rewarding experience for me to see my boy return home a happy, healthy, rejuvenated young man, freed of all the excess and self-destructive tendencies that had so surrounded his early years. I remember thinking how part of the money PG&E had paid out for all the lives they had destroyed had, at least in this case, gone to save one as well. It was a very, very good feeling.

After that, it got easier to say no to a lot of people in my life who needed to be told just that. Eric began to handle a lot of the more difficult things just the way my father would have. In fact, Eric has a lot of Dad's qualities. Because of it, he is one of only three men whose opinions have ever mattered to me. My dad was the first, Ed Masry the second, and now Eric can stake his claim to that privilege.

Oh, and you should know that if Ed felt in any way that he was being "replaced" by Eric, believe me, he *loved* this shift of power. When Eric and I were married in Hawaii, in March 1999, it was Ed who gave me away. "Here kid," he said, grinning from ear to ear as he handed me over to Eric. "She's all yours. *Good luck!*"

* * *

I have all my life looked for a man who not only understood me but who believed in me as well. I have finally found him in Eric. With his help, I am beginning to understand now what it means to be whole, to have a life based on my own existence, to be independent of the need to exist through another person's life, to live vicariously on any level, be it physical or emotional.

> "Here kid," he said, grinning from ear to ear as he handed me over to Eric. "She's all yours. Good luck!"

· ·

CHAPTER TEN

Life Will Always Be a Struggle, But You Can Win!

Whenever people ask me what I do for a living, I like to smile and say "I live." My work today continues to be about what it is I'm trying to do and to keep my message out there. I'm not an expert in much of anything, and I'm certainly not a lawyer. *I'm simply Erin Brockovich, and I have tried to make a difference in my life and in all of our lives.* I have loved sharing my story and my philosophies with you, and by doing so, I hope I've been able to prove to you that if I can do something to change our world, then so can you. Not everything you or I will do will be as newsworthy as the Hinkley case became, and there may not be as huge a monetary reward at the other end, but if you are true to yourself, and your moral and spiritual foundation remain strong and intact, you will enjoy a different and far more valuable reward. You will discover, among other things, there is no obstacle you cannot surmount, no challenge you cannot meet, no fear you cannot conquer, no matter how impossible it may sometimes seem. My life is living proof that you can dive headlong into the waters of adversity to rescue others who are caught in the rip tide of their own lives.

This past spring a wonderful thing happened to me. I was awarded an honorary master's degree in arts and business communication from the first fully accredited Internet university, Jones International, an organization that provides an opportunity for people who work full time to acquire a college degree at their own pace. Hey, this isn't so bad for a dyslexic who never finished undergraduate school. That's called *stick-to-itiveness!*

> Whenever people ask me what I do for a living, I like to smile and say, "I live."

*   *   *

I have a much greater appreciation these days for those we always refer to as an "overnight success." I can see now how easy it is for these O.S.'ers, awash in a storm of media, to lose the very sense of who they are when the spotlight has "suddenly" fallen on them, and how, in a certain ironic twist of success, the hotshot to their ego makes them something of a "failure" all over again. The key to maintaining your sanity when anything unusual happens in your life to upset your natural rhythmic flow is to try to always remember that in the end, the attention, the glare, and the money (if there is any) are not what it is "about" you that has brought all of it down on your head. Success isn't "about" any single person. At best, your actions and achievements serve as a vehicle for much greater stories, causes, and numbers of people. It is not about ego, but issues. It is not about you, but who you represent, and the success that the collective efforts of all the unseens and unknowns have collected to make you the "star" of your very own 15 minutes.

*   *   *

As for me, I have to say that my postmovie life has been a wild ride, at times enervating, at times nerve-wracking. By now, of course, I have been asked about a half-million times since the night of the Academy Awards what my reaction was to Julia's not mentioning me in her acceptance speech, and it never fails to make to me laugh. This, by the way, is *exactly* what I'm talking about. To me, Julia's winning the award was a validation of the work *we'd all done for Hinkley,* and the film helped get *our* message to a far wider audience. Just because in her confusion and excitement, she momentarily omitted my name means nothing to me. Nothing at all. In fact, I didn't even attend the awards. That night I decided instead to stay home. One

> At best, your actions and achievements serve as a vehicle for much greater stories, causes, and numbers of people.

of my children had become ill, and I didn't want to leave her alone. I was quite content for us to gather around the television like every other family in America and watch the program unwind. It was Julia's night, for sure, and it was Steven Soderbergh's night. As for me? My Academy Award was the look on the faces of the people in Hinkley when they saw the system worked. That was the only "Oscar" I ever needed.

Still, I remember the first time I heard that Julia had agreed to play me. By then Steven, the director, had already spent a considerable amount of time working with me. He said he wanted to try to pick up my inflections, my feelings and passions for things, to generally discover who I was and what I was really all about. In the meantime, Susannah Grant, the screenwriter, was trying to pare the story down, seeking to keep the focus as much on the events without making the movie such a polemic no one would want to see it.

Anyway, my very first reaction to hearing that Julia was going to play me was shock. Then I burst out laughing. All during the time the film was coming together, Ed kept on asking who I thought should play me. "I don't know," I'd say, and Ed would then pull out his list of suggestions, always headed by Sharon Stone. That *really* made me laugh. And he never failed to add, "As long as it's not Julia Roberts." Of course, he didn't mean it personally. Let's face it, he didn't believe in me either until we got to know each other.

And now, here for the record, once and for all, I think Julia did a great job in the film. Because her portrayal was so accurate, people still think we actually look alike, which is not just a great compliment to me but to her acting abilities as well.

I did, however, go to the opening of the film. I think that night was one of the most exciting evenings I have ever spent in my life. The anticipation was nearly unbearable for me, mostly because it gave me time to think about how I was going to react to seeing myself being portrayed up there on the big screen. Thankfully, I had enough time to put my ego in check. After all, there was a lot going on here that could swell my head, if I allowed it, beginning with the name of the film—*Erin Brockovich*. That was wild! Someone said to me I was about to become a household name!

Then, of course, I realized the household name wasn't really mine at all. You see, I'd kept Brockovich only because in my second divorce decree, someone had somehow managed to leave out the bit about my name changing to the one I was born with—*Erin Pattee*. When I got to the courthouse, they wanted an additional $675 to make the change, which at the time I didn't have. So I thought, hey, so what? All of this came flooding back to me that night in a very solid way because it helped remind me once again that the picture was not really all about me but about what a woman who happened to be named Brockovich had managed to accomplish with the help of a whole lot of other people. As far as I was concerned, the film could just as well have been called *Ed Masry* (although I don't think dear Albert Finney's cleavage is nearly as attractive as Julia's).

Seriously, that night the resistance to ego inflation made

something else inside of me swell, a sense of real pride and accomplishment. I had *earned* something special, and now I had a right to stand tall and say, yes, I did a good job. I remembered, amidst all the flashing bulbs and microphones, something my dad had told me when all of this started, about how the material rewards of accomplishment should not be the reason we do anything, but merely a side-product, the aftermath of the real reward, the knowledge of having done something to make another human being's life a little better.

In that light, it was an absolute privilege for me to be associated with this film, and, yes, a hoot seeing myself as others involved in the story first saw me, some big-breasted girl running around in high-heeled shoes and bustier with no legal education attempting to pull together a massive toxic tort litigation while raising three children with no husband and a male nanny. I mean, come on—Hollywood couldn't make my life up in a million years!

There were, in fact, persistent rumors that I didn't really exist at all, that I was indeed a "made-up" character, the product of some feverish producer's overactive imagination. I think that was because remarkably little had been written about the case prior to the record-breaking settlement and then the making of the film. Certainly I was anything but the household name I was about to become. Once the film opened, of course, that all changed. The next day more than 300 requests for interviews came in. I was shocked by the sheer number, and I was also relieved to know that people finally believed I wasn't a made-up character.

And ironically, the movie made me famous, an American "personality," even as it entertainingly presented the success of our exposé of the evil side of Corporate America. Steven Soderbergh always felt the film had a very strong social message, and he knew if he told it the right way, its impact would be powerful on both the political *and* emotional levels. He was right, and I'm certain that long after I'm forgotten, the real legacy of the movie will live on, and that is a very good thing.

Still, if my husband, Eric *Ellis,* is called "Mr. Brockovich" one more time, or asked, "Are you that biker dude?" he will absolutely blow a gasket!

By the night of the premiere, one of the biggest openings Universal had had in years, I'd dropped nearly 20 pounds and could no longer fit into the dress I'd chosen for this big night. I had to go instead with an old knock-off with the back cut out all the way down to the top of my butt, the front barely covering my chest. I found it in the back of my closet, and I put it on. It was snug tight. Perfect, I thought, and I told Eric I was ready.

On the drive over, I was incredibly nervous and tugged at his arm, asking over and over again like an excited little girl, "What if nobody shows up? *What if nobody shows up?*" Eric tried to calm me down, but I was hopeless. When we finally arrived, Steven was waiting to greet us. We got out of the car, and I could see people everywhere, and TV crews from *Access Hollywood, Entertainment Tonight,* all the shows. Then I noticed the famous red carpet didn't go straight into the theater. Instead, it took this circuitous route for the benefit of the public and the press. I couldn't believe it! At one point during this march through the gauntlet, Steven whispered in my ear, "How're you doing?"

I wanted to tell him that taking on PG&E was nothing compared to this! I do remember not liking my picture being taken. Someone then shouted, "Erin Brockovich is here!" and all hell broke loose. There I was smack in the middle of the media lion's den. I was ferociously pulled every which way but toward the entrance to the theater. Microphones and cameras were shoved right up close into my face. Flashbulbs went off everywhere. Talk about a Cinderella story, this was it!

Finally, after what seemed like an eternity, it was time to start the film. I was led into the packed theater where I took my seat, settled in, and waited for the lights to go down. And then, for the next two hours I watched as the events of the last 10 years of my life flickered on the screen, my spirit and my soul captured for two hours by the wondrous Julia Roberts!

It was quite a night. All my life I'd had a feeling inside that something good was going to happen to me, that I had a calling, a destiny, somewhere I was supposed to go, someone I was meant to be. When I was younger I thought for a moment or two it might happen through modeling, or acting, but those were just the fancies of a teenage dreamer. In truth, for a long time I was lost, disconnected from the fertile root of my spiritual and moral foundation. Then, slow and late-blooming for sure, I was transformed from a down-and-out single mom to a $2.5 million bonus baby, with a movie having been made about my accomplishments, and several standing-room-only motivationally themed lecture series dealing with my "Unique Life Experiences."

What I love most is getting out and meeting all the people. I've been so impressed, especially at the university level. There are so many young people who are looking and searching for the right thing to do, for some level of professional fulfillment and personal happiness in their lives. Young people want to make a difference. I see it everywhere I go. I receive hundreds of phone calls from boys and girls eighteen and under who just want to talk to me for a few minutes, to say thanks. This is, by the way, one of the best "rewards" imaginable.

I especially love talking to women's groups, discovering how many women there are out there with the desire and ability to empower themselves, to rise above the level of their socially taught self-expectations. I never try to focus on specific issues, or chemicals, or judges, or any of that. My lectures are extensions of my universal philosophy of self-belief. For instance, everything I had been taught my whole life I saw going wrong in Hinkley. There was a horrible mass lie taking place that was destroying the dignity and the value of the families there, and their health was being taken away from them. It was my desire to help these people that guided my life and caused me to rediscover my own self-worth. I learned something that I had known all along but had never applied until Hinkley. Once I connected all that I had been taught as a child with all that I saw going wrong for the people of that town, my life came together. That is the message I give during my travels across the country, a never-ending journey that has been so spiritually rewarding for me.

And the further I go, the more I remember where I started from. The more fatigued I feel from the drudge of modern-day travel, the more I am sustained by the strength of my convictions. And whenever I feel the need or intimidated by all the attention or panicky because there seems to be no end to the deluge—it's already been a year after the movie and not only has there been no letup in requests for me to speak, I'm getting more calls than ever—I sit down alone somewhere, either in a hotel if it's on the road or in my bedroom at home, make myself some tea, relax, turn off the TV and the radio, *and have a good long talk with myself.* That's when I remind myself all over again that hey, babe, all of this action is merely the sweet coating on a very *real* person called *Erin.* And then I tell myself that the things that have always been most important to me—love, family, honor, and integrity—didn't begin or end with Hinkley, the movie, or the lectures. It was all there waiting to come out, and it will be there tomorrow when I face the next major obstacle to fall onto my pathway.

That is how I keep my perspective (as well as my sanity) on all the things that have happened to me, and a sense of humor about some of the sillier things, like being offered a lot of money to pose for *Playboy,* which I turned down. I just don't see myself that way. To me, my ongoing presence is a sign that the issues I've raised and the work I've done have made a lasting impact, and that remains the most valid reason for me to continue to do what I do.

I know some women, all single, who go out every week with

a different guy. When the fellow doesn't call them back, they always start to run him down, to cite what was wrong with him and how he wasn't really "marriage material" in the first place. My reaction is always the same: It's all the *guy's* fault? The *guys* have all the problems? *Hello?* Take a look at yourself. Maybe the problem isn't them at all. Maybe it's a little closer to home than you're willing to admit. It's awfully hard for someone else to start to like you when you don't like yourself all that much.

> It's awfully hard for someone else to start to like you when you don't like yourself all that much.

Whatever happened to impressing others by acts of kindness? By demonstrations of principles, by being someone with integrity and honor? I think those qualities will take you a lot further than having your butt exposed in the pages of some magazine. Was it tempting? Sure. I'm not going to be a hypocrite and pretend that it wasn't. But I have three children to consider. And a little something I've come to cherish these last few years called *self-respect.*

*   *   *

And so I have gotten on with my life. I still work with the law firm, and I am constantly being called upon by lawyers, judges, students, and legal groups to teach them what I know about what I did. My answer to one and all about that is always the same. I can't "teach" what I didn't learn. My experience in the Hinkley case was driven by who I am, not what I learned. To my way of thinking, the law isn't black and white, it's not strictly about rules, but about the will of passion. Through my work on the Hinkley case, I have come to believe in attorneys and what they can do to make this a better world.

In that sense, the case reestablished my confidence in attorneys, even as it was reawakening my faith in myself. Any advice I can give goes far beyond the tenets of the law. All of us, not just lawyers, should remember that we are all human beings. Let's not talk above people. Try to take yourself out of your own shoes and imagine the other guy, who is sick, who maybe lost a loved one, who is no longer able to work, who can't provide for his or her family. Put yourself in that person's shoes, and try to behave with the same compassion you would have for yourself. I had more than one attorney tell me in the days, months, and years before the Hinkley settlement to "quit being so emotional," or "you're exaggerating," or "that can't be true." It used to drive me crazy. It's that kind of pompous arrogance that has always disturbed me. You want to do what I did? Feel as I felt for the next person, and you'll be feeling something for yourself. Remember, what goes around comes around. If you live with no respect for your fellow human beings, you will get none in return. I promise you that, and I speak from experience.

And for all you lawyers-to-be, for God's sake, don't go into it solely for the money. For every one trying to get into the spotlight, there is a drastic shortage of lawyers willing to go the extra mile for the disenfranchised, the lost, and the forgotten. You want to know what I know about law? Look to the latter, for they can teach you all you'll ever need to know.

On the occasion when a case does come my way whose circumstances move me to the point where I can't help but want to get involved, I simply brush aside my already impossibly overcrowded schedule and plunge in. I am currently involved in several cases, at least five of which are still in litigation today. The first month the film was in release, we had 100,000 inquiries on the Masry-Vititoe website regarding potential toxic sites. We're still receiving hundreds of e-mails and letters. Sadly, there is no end to the number of people, mostly disenfranchised, who need help and encouragement to take on the overwhelmingly powerful obstacles that threaten their very lives.

*   *   *

Hopefully, the Hinkley case will serve as a model for others caught in a similar situation. I'm not going to try to kid you or myself. Bad things happen, and not every situation resolves itself as Hinkley did, but if what we did can inspire others to *believe enough in themselves to want to try to make a difference,* then I will always feel justified in having fought the good fight, and proud of my achievements.

I also want to keep my political activities going. I want to see to it that our environmental problems are not "solved" cosmetically, so that our current president doesn't leave a 50-year legacy of natural disaster in his wake. A lot of us have to get in there and fight on a legislative level, and that group is going to include me.

I also have several TV projects in the works, including one based on a very successful British series, *Challenge Annica,* in which I would be the American version of Annica, the original host. It would be a series of specials in which we would take on some kind of challenge and meet it, utilizing the help of major organizations, foundations, and ordinary people, all of whom have the power to get things done. It's a positive, tangible variation on all the "reality" shows that are now so popular. This one isn't about prizes for contestants; it's about help for the needy. The big reward on our show will be the satisfaction for all those who get involved trying to help others who can't help themselves.

I'll also continue to lecture, to share my stories and to get my message out there. I need to try to reach people who feel power-less, to help them locate their inner strength, to reignite the beliefs they should have in themselves, to be prepared to go through whatever struggle is necessary. My message remains to stick with it, keep going, and come out on the other side a winner! If I can reach just one individual and convince him or her not to follow the antiquated rules of our society as guidelines for how to live their lives, but rather to look inside themselves for the root of their own values, then I have done my job. I'm talking about the grown-up person fighting for noble causes, but I'm also talking about the child left out of the group because he's carrying a trumpet instead of a guitar! That youngster is going to feel ostracized, will be hurt, and will lose faith in himself unless someone befriends him, encourages him, and reassures his right to be his own person. This is exactly the kind of judgment that affects us from our earliest days into adulthood and does so much personal damage. Ironically, the only way out of that is to go further inside yourself. Remember: You're never too old or too young to make a commitment to yourself—to do the things you do in life well, no matter how great or how ordinary, and to do them with integrity. The key to success is persistence to build the confidence necessary to *believe in yourself!*

And I'm living proof that this works. If I can do it, *and I did,* then you can too. So give yourself that good talking to. Look in the mirror today, and watch your own face as you convince yourself of who you really are.

*　　*　　*

I'm Erin Brockovich. I had a terrible time getting through school. I'm dyslexic. I have been divorced two times and married three times. I have discovered the true meaning of "Three times is the charm . . ." I have three children I raised with little outside child support. I have been so lonely I sat in a corner and shook. I have been scared to death. I have been very sad. I have suffered from anorexia. I have suffered from panic disorders. I have been poor, and I have been rich. I have searched my whole life to be fulfilled.

I am Erin Brockovich. I have the strength, the conviction, and moral empowerment to be who I really am.

And you are . . . ? Let's get together!

CHAPTER ELEVEN

Erin's Shorthand Guide to Winning Life's Struggles

What follows are a series of messages, a guideline really, to the way I have learned to approach the obstacles in my own life. Each one addresses a different aspect of the struggles we all face. The first direction is outer—to isolate the problem, identify the route to its obstacle, and figure out a way to get around it. The second direction (simultaneously acknowledged) is inward. This involves understanding *your reaction* to an obstacle, exploring what it is within you that strengthens it, that allows it to feed off of your own weaknesses, whatever they may be. Doing this will give you a start toward formulating your own line of attack.

Much of the essential makeup of my guidelines is a structured line of thought, meditations that have helped me align my heart with my head, my mind with my spirit, my goals with my accomplishments. Read them, learn them, use them as both shield and weapon, and they will help you better understand who you are, why you do the things you do, what the essence of your behavior is that makes you successful, or where the obstacles lie that prevent your success from happening.

What follows will not solve the problems of the world, but it may help you begin to conquer the problems of *your* world. Good luck in all your endeavors. And remember, *I am on your side.*

1. *If my heart, my gut, and my mind are not in sync, something has to be wrong* internally, *and until I fix it, I cannot attain my inner harmony.*

   Often, we misread the messages our emotions are sending us. Either we personalize a situation that is not meant to be taken as such, or we *depersonalize* exactly what it is we should be "taking to heart." Understanding the difference between these will reduce the confusion of your reaction and clarify the plan of your approach to a solution. A question I am often asked is whether or not my devotion to Hinkley was strictly business or purely emotional. The answer is complex, probably a little bit of both, as most meaningful challenges tend to

   > **If my heart, my gut, and my mind are not in sync, something has to be wrong internally, and until I fix it, I cannot attain my inner harmony.**

be. What made my focus sharper and my goals clearer was that while I *identified* with the victims, I was able to segregate my legal weapons, so that I could mount an effective two-prong attack, while preventing my sympathies and my outrage from overruling the effectiveness of my research. The bottom line is that the head and the heart do not operate separately. They work *in tandem.* The breakdown of your reaction to any obstacle or challenge will help you assign their component parts. This will allow you to react and evaluate with your moral, or emotional, side while adding strength to your intellectual, or logical, response.

This works especially well in relationship problems, where too often we allow our emotions to overwhelm us and neutralize whatever it is we can do to move forward effectively to workable solutions for lifelong happiness with the right partners for us.

2. *Lying is the deadly cancer of the emotions. It spreads through your mind and eventually kills your spirit.*

Often we think of lying as "kidding ourselves," which is like calling a malignant tumor a "benign mole." Whenever we lie to anybody else, we are really

> Lying is the deadly cancer of the emotions. It spreads through your mind and eventually kills your spirit.

lying to ourselves. Somewhere along the way, the lie will "work" and will become the truth, as you have re-created it. Once this happens, your moral guidelines, your essential honesty, the level of your integrity—all of it self-destructs and the result is that you are no longer facing your obstacles, you *are* your obstacles.

See if you can go through a single day without telling even the smallest lie. Use that as a springboard to a new level of honesty. The reward will be a stronger will to seek the truth within yourself, *about* yourself, and to identify a better approach to the solutions you seek.

3. *Do what you like, and you'll succeed.*
What is the difference between talent and ability? *Motivation.* Better to try to be the best you that you can be than the best there is. *Passion* is the key to solving this equation. Skill without talent is never going to win out over ability infused with passion. No matter what anyone else may say, think, or do, let your passion guide you in life. When it comes to career and achievement, stick with what you like, and you will be amazed at how good

> Do what you like, and you'll succeed.

you already are at it. When I first began dealing with people as a salesperson, I discovered I had an ability to make them listen, and they often bought what I was selling. It was out of that first success that I realized I had an *ability* to communicate with people, and whether or not I did well because I liked it or I liked it because I did well, the bottom line was I liked it *and* I did well. This is the combination you are looking for in order to succeed in whatever field of endeavor you choose to pursue.

4. *Be realistic about your situations and yourself.*

Everyone can't be the leader of the team. We are all created differently, and while some of us have talents that are more obvious than others, we all have a level of attainment that we can reach. Remember, it is not the size of the dog in the fight, but the size of the fight in the dog.

> Be realistic about your situations and yourself.

5. *Ego is our greatest stumbling block.*

When we think we can get away with something, it is because we think we are "smarter" or "better" than everyone else. We may be, we may not be. These are not the deciding factors in any struggle. The willingness to

> Ego is our greatest stumbling block.

try your best and fail will make your commitment that much stronger and your success that much more accessible.

6. *Strive for what you believe in.*
   Family, health, honesty. These are the tenets by which I guide my life. I strive to defend what I believe in, to search for the truth without compromising my integrity.

   > Strive for what you believe in.

7. *Seek what fulfills you.*
   We all search for true happiness. Just be careful where you look for it. If you think that material comforts are the only tickets to happiness, you will not find what you are looking for. Seek what fulfills your heart. Don't let others "sell" you objects of satisfaction. Find satisfaction through your actions toward others. The greatest reward is making a difference.

   > Seek what fulfills you.

8. *Dress for the part.*
   Why not? Life is supposed to be fun, isn't it? If people don't like it, *Tough!*

   > Dress for the part.

9. *Talk to yourself.*

Talking to yourself is one of the best ways to get to know and understand the real issues and problems that concern you. You will find you are your best listener. Take the time to sort out your issues. Go to a mirror if you have to, but talk it all out. You'll be amazed at how effective this is in helping you to understand and overcome what seem to be the most insurmountable problems. Try it. It works.

> Talk to yourself.

10. *Learn from mistakes.*

By learning from your mistakes, you will discover they are not mistakes after all. They are learning tools. Do not be afraid to fail. Failure is the best route to finding real success.

> Learn from mistakes.

11. *Honesty, integrity, persistence.*

These are the three most important qualities of life. Never let your goals in life or desires make you compromise these values. Any victory is meaningless without them.

> Honesty, integrity, persistence.

12. *Love yourself!*

Love yourself for who you are, not who you one day hope to be. Stay focused on the alignment of your spirit, your soul, your mind, and your heart. These are the ingredients of your being,

Love yourself!

and they will lift you to the best place you can be in your life. Happiness is first found in the attempt.

13. *The time is* now!

Not long ago, I received a phone call from the daughter of a female attorney I had met during the extortion case. The attorney, Kathleen Drury, was a strong woman who provided me with a lot of strength, and she became a close friend and

The time is now!

confidante. About three months ago, she developed what she thought was a sinus infection that turned out to be a brain tumor. She never let anybody know how serious it really was. She had surgery, and we were told they had gotten all of the cancer. Her daughter called later on to tell me she had died. It's the same familiar hard lesson, perhaps the most important of all. One day you're here, and the next day you're gone. We sometimes forget how wonderful we are as people, and how precious and extraordinary—and transient—is the gift of life. I'd love to see that feeling restored. I cherish the opportunity to love my friends. Too often, we get caught up in our chaos and forget to do this. Kathleen's death is the hard reminder of what is really important in our lives. Take the time to tell your loved ones just that, that they are your loved ones. Stop for a moment during the day and let the sun bathe your face. Take a second or two to listen to the music of the laughter of your children as they play. Go to a river bank and listen to the sound of the water, the chirping of birds, the blowing of the wind. It is the world around you that speaks to you, that will inspire you. If you listen hard enough, you will find the voice within yourself, and the ability and the power to make a difference.

Take it from me: You can do it all!

Acknowledgments

First and foremost, I want to thank my mother and father and the rest of my immediate family. Mom and Dad, words can't express the love I have for you. How does one say "thank you" for the foundation you provided upon which I built my hopes and dreams, and realized them? You instilled within me the courage to become the person I am today. There will always be a special place in my heart for my brother Tommy, the pied piper of our family, whom I so dearly miss, as well as for my talented sister, Jodie, and for brother Frank, the "great philosopher." And, of course, my children, Matthew, Katie, and Elizabeth, all of whom I unconditionally adore, and who have shared so much of the rough go of these years with me. I only hope I have been able to pass on to them what my parents gave me, the ability to believe in themselves and stand on their own. We stuck together, kids. We're the team; you're my star players!

I want to thank my husband, Eric, for sharing with me the mutual respect, love, and support throughout it all. You came into my life through the eye of the storm and never blinked. Through everything that went down, you stood up better than the rest. You not only took me on but my two teenage children too, who were not doing so well at the time, and my youngest daughter, your little pride and joy. And you also managed to deal with the craziness of the whole movie thing. I love you.

I want to thank Ed and Joette Masry and Jim and Karen Vititoe. You are all heroes to me. Your generosity was incredible. It was the four of you, collectively, who decided to share with me in the adventure of my life, who so profoundly impacted not only me but my children as well. No acknowledgment can truly express the feelings I have for you, Ed. And Jim, I will never forget that this all started with you.

I want to thank Pamela Dumond, the chiropractor who first heard the details of my life and thought there must be a movie in there somewhere. You are a great lady, a dear friend, a wonderful healer. Thanks for sharing my stories!

I want to thank Carla Schamberg, the executive producer of the movie. You have a great sense of yourself as a woman and a person. You grabbed hold and believed in me and have an incredible sense of passion and justice. You are one of the few women I've known whose life is a total representation of everything I stand for. Also, the rest of Jersey Films, especially Michael Schamberg, Carla's husband, Stacey Sher, and Danny DeVito. Danny, you are clearcut and have such a great love of family. Also Universal Pictures, the legendary Albert Finney, and of course, the great Julia Roberts. You, Julia, were the power name that brought the film to life. Susannah Grant, the screenwriter, another strong female, you have a great sense of yourself, and you are filled with honor, and family, and Steven Soderbergh, the director. Steven, you are a man of immense talent and compassion. You "got" what Hinkley was all about. To all of you, you are the group that helped show America there are great people out there, like Ed Masry, who run corporations and are also human and compassionate and have enough belief in themselves to allow "nobodies" to come to the plate and take their swing at the ball—so people like Roberta Walker, Lillian Melendez, and Chuck Ebersohl can become empowered and make a difference in the world in which we live. Roberta, I don't know where any of us would be today had it not been for you. Lillian, there is no one like you. My life is better for having known you. Chuck, thank you.

I want to thank Kim Redmond, who has been like a second mother, and her daughter, Brynne. These people have been an extended family for me in my many absences.

I want to thank my dear friend Kathy Brown, whom I adore and who is another of the strong, affirmative women of this world.

I want to thank Kathy Borseath, the teacher who helped me get through high school, recognized my condition, and helped me try to get over it. I am certain she has no idea what an enormous difference she made in my life. Nevertheless, she was crucial to the development of my sensibilities.

I also want to acknowledge that Shawn, Steve, and Jorge will form their own opinions about this book, if they read it. The story I have told is not intended to hurt any of them. Rather, they are a part of my history, and the experiences I had with them helped me become the person I am today.

I want to thank Chris Newman, Mark Itkin, Betsy Berg, and Mel Berger of the William Morris Agency. Chris and Mark are in Beverly Hills, Betsy handles my lecture series, and Mel is in New York on the literary end of things. I also want to thank the agency for putting me together with Marc Eliot, my writing collaborator, my partner in crime! Marc, I hold you in a special place, right up there with Ed, Eric, and my dad. Thanks for sitting in the sun and for having the patience to sit and listen to all I had to say, in between chasing the birds. I couldn't have done this without you.

I want to thank Mary E. Glenn, my editor at McGraw-Hill for believing in and sharing in my thoughts and philosophies. Mary, you have enabled me to extend my ideas to the public.

And of course I want to thank you, dear reader, for listening to my message. Good luck to every one of you!

About the Authors

Erin Brockovich is the real-life inspiration for the Oscar-winning movie that bears her name. Today, she continues to do legal work as a director of environmental research and is involved in consulting on numerous toxic waste investigations. Brockovich is active on the motivational speaking circuit, with a thriving lecture series and a television talk show in development. She lives in Los Angeles, California.

Marc Eliot is the *New York Times* best-selling author of several biographies and books on popular culture, including *Down 42nd Street, The Whole Truth, Death of a Rebel, Down Thunder Road,* and *Rockonomics*. He has cowritten with Barry White, Vicki Lawrence, Roy Clark, and others, and divides his time between Hollywood and New York City.

And One More Thing . . . About Those Dolphins

Why have I chosen to feature the dolphin symbol throughout the design of my book? I love dolphins. They not only symbolize clean water and a clean environment, to me they also represent freedom, love, respect, the ability to communicate, and the desire to stand up for and protect one another. Dolphins travel in pods and become much like an extended family—brothers, sisters, cousins. I'm reminded of the saying, "It takes a village to raise a child." Dolphins are such a representation of that village. One of the mother dolphins could be sick, and a sister or an aunt in the pod will come in and take care of her baby. That is so neat! I'm in awe of them. They are intelligent beyond our understanding. I think their souls speak through their eyes, and that is how I connect with them spiritually.